# Experimental And Practical Views Of The Atonement

## Octavius Winslow

# EXPERIMENTAL AND PRACTICAL

# VIEWS

# ATONEMENT.

### BY OCTAVIUS WINSLOW,
PASTOR OF THE SECOND BAPTIST CHURCH, BROOKLYN,
NEW YORK.

"The Precious blood of Christ." 1 Peter 1. 19.
"He that believeth on the Son of God, hath the witness
in himself." 1 John 5. 10.

## NEW YORK
## JOHN S. TAYLOR,
Theological and Sunday School Bookseller, Brick Church Chapel,
corner of Park Row and Spruce Street, opposite the
City Hall.

1838

TO

MY BELOVED AND REVERED

MOTHER,

Through whose early instructions and prayers,

I am indebted, under GOD,

For my first acquaintance with, and for many of my

maturer views of,

The blessed doctrine, it is an humble attempt to unfold,

THIS VOLUME

Is respectfully and gratefully

INSCRIBED

By her affectionate and dutiful

Son,

THE AUTHOR.

# PREFACE.

THIS unpretending little volume forms the commence-
ment of a series of similar works which it is the author's
design, should the Lord permit, to publish upon the important subject of experimental religion, under the general title
of, "EXPERIMENTAL AND PRACTICAL VIEWS OF DIVINE
TRUTH." Various considerations, to one or two of which,
he may be permitted to allude, suggested the undertaking,
and pleaded for its execution. The first that may be mentioned was, the vast and solemn *importance* of the subject.

The religion of the Lord Jesus is valuable only as its
power is experienced in the heart. In this respect, and in
this only, it may be compared to the physical sciences
which, however ingenious in structure, or beautiful in
theory ; yet if not reduced or reducable to purposes of
practical use, are of little worth. It is so with the truth
of Jesus. The man of mere taste may applaud its external beauty—the philosopher may admire its philosophy,
the orator its eloquence, and the poet its poetry, but if the
Spirit of GOD take not HIS own truth and impress it upon the
heart, as to the great design of its revelation, it avails nothing. What numbers are there who rest in the mere theory
of Christianity. As a practical principle they know nothing
of it. As a thing experienced in the heart, it is a hidden
mystery to them. They speak well of it as a religious

1*

system—believe its Divinity, and even defend its doctrines
and extol its ethics: yet, make no approaches towards a
personal and practical obedience to its claims.  In a word,
they know nothing of repentance towards God, and faith
towards our Lord Jesus Christ.  It will surely appear to a
spiritually enlightened mind, a subject of vast and solemn
moment. that, this delusion should be exposed—that, this
foundation of sand should be undermined, and the absolute
necessity of experimental religion, as necessary to an ad-
mission within the kingdom of glory, be strenuously and
scripturally enforced.

  Another consideration which had its weight with the
author's mind was, the conviction that the state of the
church demanded a more spiritual, experimental and practical exhibition of Divine truth.  To those who have been
silent, though sad, spectators of the recent history of the
American Church, it is known that controversies of an
alarming character have, for a lengthened period, existed
in her bosom.  They have seen and deplored the divisions
that have rent her—the party feeling that has been engen-
dered, the alienation and distance that have existed among
those who holding one Head, should therefore, "love as
brethren."  To mitigate this alarming evil, to heal these
divisions, and to draw the different sections of the church
more closely together, various able disquisitions have been
written, many ingenious plans have been proposed, and
many affecting appeals have been made.  But, it is the
author's honest conviction that, the first and the chief step
towards the accomplishment of an end so earnestly to be
sought, and so fervently to be prayed for, is to, *deepen the*

*spirituality* of the churches of each evangelical denomination. Nothing short of this will bring it about. Vain will be all expectation of returning to an Apostolic union—fruitless will be every plan for a coalition of sects while the spirituality of the church is at so low an ebb. But, augment the true piety of the churches—hold up a more elevated standard of holiness—let them be deeply baptized in the reviving and sanctifying influences of the Holy Spirit, and these controversies will all terminate, these divisions will all be healed, and the din and the strife of party interests will speedily be hushed. Christians will not hold less firmly, and defend less zealously their conscientious views of truth, but they will hold and speak the truth *in love*. In order then thus to strengthen the tone of spirituality among the churches, *experimental* and *practical* religion must be more frequently and earnestly insisted upon. There cannot possibly exist genuine piety apart from experimental truth, and in proportion to the deep experience of the truth, will be the depth of spirituality.

It will suffice to mention but one other consideration which influenced the author in the preparation of these works, and that was, the demand which the church herself has made for writings of this class. The church is wearied with controversy. There is a restlessness, a growing desire for publications of a less polemical and more spiritual and experimental character, which it is important should be met. There are those, and the number is increasing, who are hungering and thirsting for the simple truth of God, broken up and presented to them unmixed with the bitter herbs of controversy and discussion. They want

God's truth as it is.   They want it so opened and explain-
ed as to meet the daily experience of the christian life.—
The inward and the outward conflicts—the deep affliction,
the heavy cross, all of which demand an experimental unfolding of the doctrines and truths of the Bible.   And
there is a sweetness and preciousness in Divine truth thus
exhibited, which controversy tends much to impair.   The
father of the inductive philosophy, truly and beautifully
remarks, "As those wines which flow from the first tread-
ing out of the grapes, are sweeter and better than those
forced out of the press, which gives the roughness of the
husk and of the stone; so are those doctrines best and
wholesomest which flow from a gentle crush of the Scriptures, and are not wrung into controversies."*

To meet in some degree this demand, has been the humble attempt of the author.   How far he has proved suc-
cessful, the experienced believer must decide.   He has
commenced with the doctrine of the Atonement of Christ,
it being the central truth of the Bible, on which all others
are based, and around which they all entwine.   The second volume in the series will embrace "EXPERIMENTAL
AND PRACTICAL VIEWS OF THE WORK OF THE HOLY
SPIRIT, and will appear, should the author's life and health
be preserved, early in the ensuing autumn.   Should the
Lord, in a solitary instance, condescend to bless the pe-
rusal of this work, let all the praise and the glory redound
to the Father, Son, and Holy Ghost. the Triune Jehovah,
to whom it alone belongs.                          O. W.

BROOKLYN, N. Y. April, 1838.

---

* Bacon.

# CONTENTS.

## INTRODUCTION.

The Province of Reason in the investigation of
Spiritual and Experimental Truth  -   -   - 13

## CHAPTER I.

The Spiritual and Experimental Character of the
Atonement : Inexplicable to the Unregenerate  - 32

## CHAPTER II.

The Atonement in its relation to the Godhead of
Christ  -   -   -   -   -   -   -   - 46

## CHAPTER III.

The Speciality of the Design of the Atonement  - 90

## CHAPTER IV.

The Freeness of the Atonement -   -   -   - 160

CONTENTS.

## CHAPTER V.

The Sympathy of the Atonement -　-　-

## CHAPTER VI.

The Fearful Alternative of Rejecting the Aton
ment　-　-　-　-　-　-　-

# EXPERIMENTAL AND PRACTICAL

# VIEWS

OF

# DIVINE TRUTH.

---

## I.—THE ATONEMENT.

# INTRODUCTION.

## THE PROVINCE OF REASON IN THE INVESTI-
## GATION OF SPIRITUAL AND EXPERI-.
## MENTAL TRUTH.

*"The world by wisdom knew not God."*—1 Cor. i. 21.

In a few observations, intended mainly as in-
troductory to this series of works, we wish to
explain what we believe to be the legitimate
province of Natural Reason in the investigation
of revealed truth. We feel the more impelled
to this—perhaps otherwise unnecessary task—
least in the views we may advance on experimental religion, we shall be suspected of abro-
gating entirely the exercise of the intellectual
faculties in the study and experience of God's
truth, thus turning away from a most important
instrument which He has given us for the
purpose of weighing and sifting the evidence of
its validity.

The two extremes towards which writers on

2

Christianity have verged, have been, the opponents of the system on the one hand, discanting upon the power and sufficiency of reason, as though all the light which we possess of the invisible world and its sublime realities, were owing to its discoveries, and to no other source: and on the other, the advocates of the system, abdicating almost entirely the employment of our mental faculties—setting aside the use of reason, assigning to it no office, and awarding to it no distinction. Both, we believe to be in error; each extreme of opinion untenable. The one, in elevating reason too high, the other, in depressing it too low. The one, in investing us with the prerogative of GOD, the other, in robbing us of the dignity of man. We feel it important then briefly and in simple terms, to state what province should be assigned to human reason in prosecuting our researches in revealed and experimental truth. And that the reader may have the subject clearly before him, we shall first show what is *not*, and then what *is*, the proper use of reason in matters of religious faith.

*First*, it is not the province of human reason to *discover* spiritual truth. This far transcends

the power of the highest created reason, unenlightened by the Spirit of GOD. We do not say
that the mind taught of GOD, can discover nothing
of the glory of His character, the excellence and
loveliness of Jesus, and the spirituality and fitness of His truth. By no means would we assert
this. The mind Divinely illuminated can penetrate deeply into the vast domain of faith, and
discover the glories there revealed. But without this teaching, aside from this Divine illumi-
nation, it cannot advance a step. All is dark,
all mysterious. And just what the telescope is
to the eye of the astronomer, as when with a
glance, he sweeps the firmament of nature in
search of new and undiscovered worlds, faith is
to the eye of reason as it ranges the firmament
of revelation in search of the glorious truths of
GOD. But unenlightened by the Holy Spirit, it
can discover nothing. Take, for example, the
existence, perfections, and moral government of
Jehovah, what can human reason discover here?
What light can it throw upon the fundamental
article of our belief,—the being of GOD? Our
*senses* may assure us that we exist. That we
form but a moiety of human existence is equally

certain. That we have existed but a short time, *memory* testifies ;—and that we are not self-created, but that there must be a First Cause from which all creation originated, is all that we can deduce from these obvious facts. This is the utmost limit to the discoveries of reason. "*Who* is this First Cause?" "*What* is He?" "*Where* is He?" "In what relation does He stand to me?" "How may I propitiate His regard, and be admitted to communion with Him?" are momentous questions on which reason may *conjecture*, but on which it can pronounce with no authority.

Let the reader glance but for a moment at the *results* to which reason has come in its investigation of religious truth. What are they? where is the evidence of its mighty powers? where is the scribe? where is the philosopher? where is the disputer of this world? let them produce the amount of their researches. What discoveries have they made of GOD? what light have they reflected upon His moral attributes? How far have they penetrated into the dark and deep abyss of futurity, demonstrating with certainty whether there be *any* state after this, and

if there be, what that state is? How have they
accounted for the existence of moral evil? and
what balm have they proposed for the mitigation
of all its entailed miseries? And how have they
solved the problem, that God can be a just
God—just to His law, just to Himself, and yet
be the justifier of the *ungodly?* We ask, and are
referred to tradition, while that tradition is derived, we are all assured, from the fountain of
divine revelation.

That this is not mere assertion, unsustained
by evidence, let us show.   No fact is more certain, then that, all the knowledge which the ancient philosophers had of morals and of God,
was traditionary; revelation being the source of
that tradition.   We may enquire in the language
of Turtullian, " which of the poets, which of the
sophists was there, who did not drink of the
prophet's fountain?" To this they came wearied
with their own fruitless researches, and panting
for some better guide than reason.  Here they
drank, Ovid from Moses, and Virgil from Isaiah
Another of the Fathers styles Plato the *Hebrew
Philosopher*, while a third asserts that, from the
Hebrew writings, he derived his pious conceptions

2*

of GOD and His worship. A heathen writer
asserts that, Pythagorus transferred many things
from the Jewish institutions into his own philosophy, and styles him the imitator of the Jewish
dogmas ; and it is certain from the testimony of
Hermippus, as quoted by Selden and Grotius,
that Pythagorus dwelt among the Jews and
must necessarily have been familiar with their
religion. Another heathen writer was often heard
to ask the question, "What is Plato but Moses
atticizing ?" And who can doubt but the *lo on*
of this philosopher, was borrowed from the I AM
of Moses ; and that his *nous logos* and *psuke
cosmo*, clearly refer to the Word and the Spirit,
by whom, as he learned from the Old Testament,
the world was made. Thus it is evident from
the few examples cited, and these are not all
that might be adduced in proof of the position,
that in the vast domain of spiritual truth, reason
can never assert its claims to the power of *discovery*. All it can do, is to seize upon existing
facts, and from these facts proceed to argue and
establish its conclusions.

Nor is it the province of our intellectual faculties to judge in matters of religious faith with

*an authoritative power of dictation*—rejecting
what may be inexplicable to reason, and receiving
only what is "perfectly consentaneous with
reason." There is much of deep mystery in
revelation. GOD, considered both in Himself
and in His operations, is a mystery stretching
far beyond the sublimest power of finite reason.
" Canst thou by searching find out God? canst
thou find out the Almighty unto perfection."
Job. xi. 7. And of His operations, may we not
exclaim with the same inspired penman, " Lo
these are parts of His ways; but how little a
portion is heard of Him?" xxvi. 14. Christ, too,
is the " great mystery of godliness." Whether
His complex *person* is regarded—the union of
the divine and human natures in one;—or
whether we look at His *work*—His obedience
and death constituting a full Atonement to
Divine Justice in behalf of the sins of His people,
it must be acknowledged a depth too profound for
human thought adequately to fathom. What
can poor finite reason accomplish here? What
beams can its feeble flickering light cast upon this
world of mystery? And if ever it stands forth
invested in its own native impotence, it is when

it sits in judgment upon the doctrines and facts
of revelation, discarding or retaining such
only as are intelligible to its dwarfish capacity.
" Which things," says the Apostle, " the Angels
desire to look into." Mark his expressions! He
represents not these celestial beings of purity
and intellect, as scaling the heights and diving
into the depths of redemption's mystery—but
" which things the Angels desire," scarcely dare,
but " *desire* to look into." And yet for fallen and
unrenewed mind to sit in judgment upon God's
truth, can only be exceeded in its temerity by
the depravity which prompts it.

If the truth of God, in its doctrines and facts,
is a mystery incomprehensible to unrenewed
reason, what shall we say of the truth *as experienced in the heart?* If reason cannot understand the vast frame-work of truth, how can it
comprehend the secret power by which it oper-
ates? The very fact, that, to be understood, it
must be experienced, accounts for the difficulty.
The transforming operation of the Holy Spirit
upon the mind,—giving it a new bias, new in-
clinations; turning its darkness into light, and
kindling its enmity into love. The life of God

in the soul, creating the man anew in Christ
Jesus,—that life which is hidden, ever produc-
ive of a holy life that is seen,—its hopes and
ts fears; its defeats and its triumphs—the
causes which operate to deaden it, and the spiritual nourishment by which it is supported, all,
all is incomprehensible to human reason. Truly
" the world knoweth us not."

It will be perceived then, that we readily admit that, in the revelation of God, there is much
that towers above human reason, but which is
yet perfectly agreeable to the very reason it
transcends. Is it then, we ask, the province of
our intellectual faculties to pronounce with a dic-
tatorial and authoratative tone, what matters of
religious faith shall be received and what rejected? By no means. There are mysteries
in the world of mind which philosophy cannot
unravel, why not reject them? There are mysteries in the physical world, with which reason
cannot cope, why not reject them? Our being
too is a mystery, why not, on the same grounds,
reject it, and deny our very existence? We
assert then, that the proper jurisdiction of our
reason in matters of faith and of Divine revela-

tion, does not extend so far, as that a doctrine should be rejected, merely because it is interlaced with difficulties which our intellectual faculties cannot unravel.

It is important that we devote a moment to an enquiry into the *cause* of this incapacity of reason in its natural state, to comprehend spiritual and experimental truth. The cause is, *the corruption and perversion of our reason by sin.* Sin has impaired our mental faculties—enslaved, clouded, and debased our reason. On this account, and on this only, the door is closed which leads into the great arcanum of spiritual and experimental truth. This view perfectly accounts with the spiritual delineation of man by nature. We open God's Word, and it declares, that since the fall, the nature of man has been corrupt, and his reason blind ;—his understanding darkened, and his heart, the seat of his affections, polluted. " Having the understanding darkened, being alienated from the life of God through the ignorance that is in them, because of the blindness of their heart." Eph. iv. 18. " That upon the face of the whole earth there is none that understandeth and seeketh after

God." Rom. iii. 11. The natural man, while in that state, so far from being able to explore the wide domain of spiritual truth, hates and flees from it, when proposed to his consideration, "receiving not the things of the Spirit of God, they being foolishness unto him." 1 Cor. ii. 14. This being the state of man, God's Word consequently declares it necessary that, before spiritual truth can be understood, he should be "transformed by the renewing of his mind." Rom. xii. 2.—That he should be restored to that sound mind, and enlightened understanding, and spiritual discernment, with which his nature was endowed when it came originally from the hands of God. In a word, that he should be born again, created anew in Christ Jesus; that old things should pass away, and that all things should become new. Then, and then only, will he be able to understand the "truth of God in a mystery."

From this dark and corrupted state of natural reason, arises the constant and fearful *perversion* of God's holy truth by ungodly minds, "It is the design of corrupted reason," as Dr. Owen, truly observes, "to debase all the glorious

myeteries of the gospel, and all the concernments
of them.    There is nothing in the whole mystery
of godliness, from the highest crown of it, which
is the person of Christ, ' God manifested in the
flesh ;' unto the lowest and nearest effect of his
grace, but it labours to deprave, dishonour, and
debase.    The Lord Christ, it would have in his
whole person to be but a mere man, in his
obedience and suffering to be but an example,
in his doctrine, to be confined unto the capacity
and comprehension of carnal reason, and the
holiness which he communicates by the sanctification of his Spirit, to be but that moral virtue
which is commom among men as the fruit of
their own endeavours."*

We promised to show, and in a few words,
what *is* the legitimate province of reason in the
investigation of spiritual truth.    That our intellectual faculties are to be laid aside when we
come to the study of GOD's holy Word ;—that
reason must be entirely sacrificed to faith, we
believe GOD has no where demanded.    ' Come
let us *reason* together,' is His own condescending
invitation. Isa. i. 18.—" And when Paul stood

* Owen's Work's, vol. II, p. 235.

before Felix the Roman governor, he "*reasoned* of righteousness, temperance and of a judgment to come." Acts, xxiv. 25. And in writing to the scattered Christians, the apostle Peter exhorts them to be ready always to " give an answer to every one that asketh them a *reason* of the hope that was in them, with meekness and fear." 1 Pet. iii. 15. The revelation of God asks not the surrender of our reason as a sacrifice on the altar of faith : all it demands is, that reason shall carefully, candidly, and prayerfully examine the evidence of its validity; for " if she have not satisfactory evidence of this, she cannot, without criminal rashness, surrender her own authority which the Creator had invested her with, for the government and guidance of man," and then bow humbly, reverentially, and obediently to the Word of God. This is the legitimate province of reason, when it comes to the study and examination of God's truth. Beyond this, it dare not, it cannot pass without setting in the place of GOD, and exalting itself above all that is called GOD. When God speaks plainly, it is the privilege of reason instantly to obey ; where He sees proper to throw a veil of mystery over some of His

3

revelations, it is the *duty* of reason instantly to submit, and believe what GOD has said, because GOD has said it. Mistake not then, reader, the true province of your reasoning faculties when GOD's Word speaks. He has empowered you to investigate well and thoroughly the grounds of your faith—at the same time withholding from you all authority to erect your reason as a *rule of judgment*, discarding or retaining doctrines propounded for your belief, as they may or may not accord with its taste, or capacity of comprehension. The enlightened reader will be gratified, if we once more fortify our position with the testimony of a divine, so spiritual and profound, as Dr. Owen. "To say," are his words, "that a man is not to use his reason in finding out the sense and meaning of the propositions wherein the truths of religion are represented unto him, and in judging of their truth and falsehood by the rule of them, which is the scripture, is to deny that indeed we are men, and to put a re-reproach upon our mortality, by intimating that men do not, cannot, nor ought to do, that which they not only know they do, but also that they cannot but do. For they do but vainly deceive themselves who suppose, or rather dream, that they make any determination of what is true or false in religion, without the use and exercise of their reason; it is to say they do it as beasts, and not as men; than which nothing can be spoken more to the dishonour of religion, nor more effectual to deter men from the entertainment of it. For our parts we rejoice in this, that we dare avow the religion we profess to be highly rational, and that the most mysterious articles of it are proposed unto our belief on grounds of the most unquestionable reason, and such as cannot be rejected without a contradiction to the most benign dictates of that intellectual nature wherewith of GOD we are endued. And it is not a few trifling instances of some men's abuse of their reason in its prejudiciate exercises about the things of GOD, that shall make us ungrateful to GOD that he hath made us men, or to neglect the laying out of the best that he hath intrusted us with by nature, in his service in the work of grace.*

The subject we have thus, but imperfectly,

* Owen's Work's, vol. xviii. p. 439.

discussed, speaks pointedly and solemnly to those
who are setting up their reason in opposition to
God's truth. Reader, are you such a one? pause,
before you advance another step, "least haply
you be found to fight against God!" Dare you
reject any single doctrine, or fact of revelation,
because it transcends, in its sublimity and mystery, the finite powers of your mind? What
astounding temerity is this! Dare you turn your
back upon God's truth—and in rejecting any
part of His truth, remember you turn your back
upon God Himself—dare you withhold the obedience of your faith, the homage of your affections, the entire consecration, to His service, of
your life, because there are parts of His Word
which you cannot harmonize, doctrines which
you cannot comprehend—and operations of His
moral government which accord not with your
rule of judgment, and your views of equity and
of mercy? what fearful presumption is this!
what are you? the infant of a day! and will you
oppose your puny intellect to the mind of God!
Even were the grasp of your intellect that of an
angel, yet, when measured with God's, what
is it? what too, are all your literary and scien-

tific attainments—the wisdom of ages, which you
may have toiled to accumulate; the treasures
with which you have enriched and garnished
your mind;—what is it all, but foolishness with
God? Yea, more than this,—is not the very intellect God has given you, and which He sustains, turned into a weapon of attack against His
truth? How then can you escape the woe pro-
nounced upon him, who "striveth with his
Maker."

The reader, whose eye traces this page, may
be longing to know and experience the truth,
but to the present, has "stumbled at the word"
through a desire to understand what GOD has
not revealed. Is it so? then tear yourself away
from every thing that would keep you from the
cross of Christ. To that cross you must come
as a poor, ignorant, humble sinner. You must
stand, as stood the publican; and you must cry
as did he, "GOD be merciful to me a sinner."
That depraved heart of yours must be changed;
that proud intellect must be humbled; that rebellious will must be subdued, before you can
know "the blessedness of the man, whose transgression is forgiven, whose sin is covered." Ps.

xxxii. 1. Listen to the solemn words of the Son
of God;—"Except ye be converted and become
as little children, ye shall not enter into the
kingdom of heaven." Matt. viii. 3. Listen to
the word of the Apostle; "Let no man deceive
himself. If any man among you seemeth to be
wise in this world, let him become a fool that
he may be wise. For the wisdom of this world
is foolishness with God : for it is written, He
taketh the wise in his own craftiness." 1 Cor.
iii. 18, 19. Are you longing to know the truth?
then come : the heart of GOD bids you come;
every promise of His word bids you come; and
taking your place low at the feet of Jesus, receive
with the simplicity, docility, and ingenuousness
of a child, the precious word of GOD. O lay
aside your cavilling, your false reasoning, which
does but keep you back from simply receiving
Christ as the Saviour of sinners; and impressed
with a deep and abasing sense of your ignorance
and vileness, let your ardent prayer be, "That
which I know not, teach thou me. Lead me in
thy truth, and teach me, for thou art the God of
my salvation." Job, xxxiv. 32. Ps. xxv. 5. The
reader is earnestly requested, to make this pe-

n his own, and breath it at the mercy seat,
re he passes to the next chapter, in which
 principles broached in this introduction, are
y carried out, and individually applied.

# CHAPTER I.

## THE SPIRITUAL AND EXPERIMENTAL CHARACTER OF THE ATONEMENT: INEXPLICABLE TO THE UNREGENERATE MIND.

### THE NATURE AND NECESSITY OF THE NEW BIRTH ILLUSTRATED.

"The natural man receiveth not the things of the Spirit of God, for they are foolishness unto him; neither can he know, because they are spiritually discerned." 1 Cor. ii. 14.

By no stronger argument does the truth of God establish the Divinity of its origin, than, that to all, save the regenerate, it is a sublime mystery. Not only the great principles of truth are inexplicable, but the hidden and transforming operation of that truth upon the mind,—the alarm, the contrition, the joy, the hope, the varied and often conflicting emotions which are its proper results, all, are perfectly unintelligable. The life of God in the soul, the mode of its communication, the peculiarity of its actings, and the source of its nourishment, are incomprehensible. To such an unregenerate individual, spiritual truth has no attraction. There is neither admiration of its external form, taste for its intrinsic excellence, sympathy with its holy revelations, nor love for its adorable Author. Is this a hard saying ? We fear not to assert, that to a mind on whom the renewing influence of the Holy Ghost had never passed, the great mystery of godliness is *invisible*. "Except a man be born again, he cannot *see* the kingdom of GOD." If we are to understand our Lord, whose words we quote, to mean by "the kingdom of GOD," (as the same phraseology in parallel passages would seem to decide,) not strictly the kingdom of glory and purity in which Jehovah reigns with an immediate and majestic presence, but distinctly and emphatically that spiritual empire which Christ came to establish among men, then it is as true as the testimony of Jesus can make it, that until a man is regenerated, or born from above,—until he is the subject of a new spiritual creation, the truth of GOD he cannot see. It requires no laboured process of reasoning to establish the proposition, so simple and self-evident is it—things that are spiritual

can only be discerned by a mind that is spiritual.
For instance, there is a beautiful and perfect *symmetry* in the vast structure of God's truth. Each
doctrine and precept has its proper and appropriate place.   Now how is this symmetry to be
seen ;—how is this harmonious relation and nice
adjustment of each part to the whole, to be ascertained by a mind  not only morally blind to the
truth, but all whose faculties are warring against
it ?   As well  may you  pour  tones of delicious
music on the ear of the deaf, or floods of brilliant
light on the eye-ball of the blind, and expect to
awaken  corresponding sympathy in the soul, as
that spiritual truth when brought in contact with
a " carnal mind," will produce conviction in favour either of its excellence or its beauty.   Of
the law of God,—the great asserter and defender
of the holiness of God, it is totally ignorant ;
what then does it know  of sin ? Of sin,—the
transgression of that law, its great aggravation,
its moral turpitude, it is as equally insensible ;
what then does it know of sin's wonderous Sacrifice ?   And, being ignorant of Christ, what does it
know of God ?   We repeat the observation then,
in order to  impress it upon every mind, that the

supreme excellence, and perfect harmony which pervades the entire revelations of GOD, can only be discerned by a spiritual eye.  And all this process, be it known—this heart to love the truth, this mind to investigate its nature, this eye to trace its proportions and its beauties, is the production of GOD Himself.

Expanding this thought yet further, we would dare assert, painful as it may be to the minds of many whose eye may trace this page, that he alone is a truly confirmed believer in a divine revelation, who is a true experimental believer in the Atonement of Christ.  We are prepared to admit that, there are individuals who have closely investigated and accurately weighed the external and historical evidences in corroboration of the truth of Christianity, and who, upon the conviction produced by those evidences, have received it as a system from GOD.  And yet there is a species of evidence; the nature of which they may have never examined, and the force of which they may have never felt.  The evidence to which we allude, is the *evidence of experience*, for in the striking language of GOD's own truth, " he that believeth hath the witness in himself." The Spirit of God breaking, humbling, healing the heart; taking His own truth and transcribing it upon the soul; witnessing, sealing, sanctifying; opening the eye of the soul to the holiness of God's law, to its own moral guilt, poverty, helplessness, and deep need of Christ's blood and righteousness, thus leading it to rest on Him as on an all sufficient Saviour, thus producing " righteousness, peace and joy in the Holy Ghost"—this is the truth experienced— this is the religion of the heart—and all other religion, beautiful as may be its theory, and orthodox as may be its creed, is nothing worth! Without this experience there is no true belief in God's Word. The revelation of God asks not for a faith that will merely endorse its Divine credentials. It asks not merely that scepticism will lay aside its doubts, and receive it as a Divine verity; it asks, yea it demands, more than this;—it demands a faith that will fully, implicitly, practically receive the momentous and awful facts it announces.—A faith that brings them home with a *realizing* power to the soul, and identifies it with them. A faith that believes there is a hell and seeks to escape it—

a faith that believes there is a heaven and strives to enter it. A faith that credits the doctrine of man's ruin by nature, and that welcomes the doctrine of man's recovery by grace. In a word, a faith that rejects all human dependence, and accepts as its only ground of refuge, " the righteousness of Christ, which is unto all, and upon all them that believe." O this is the true faith of the gospel! Have you it reader?

Let us for a moment glance at the different reception of God's truth by a *renewed* mind. To such an individual there is glory, harmony and exellence in spiritual truth. Every part to him is precious. No portion undervalued. In whatever form it presents itself, whether doctrinal or preceptive—with whatever tone it speaks, whether it rebukes or comforts, admonishes or cheers, he welcomes it as GOD's own eternal truth, more precious to him than gold, yea, than much fine gold. In his eye, it is a perfect system; dismember it of any one part, and you mar its beauty. It is a soverign panacea, take out of it any single ingredient, and you impair its efficacy. He must have it with no doctrine dissevered, with no precept diluted, with no insti-

4

tution perverted. He can consent to no compromise. He has bought the truth, and the truth
he cannot sell. Not only does he feel bound to
watch it with a jealous and vigilant eye, because
it is GOD's own truth, but he loves it for its
perfect adaptation to his own case. It has dis-
closed to him his sinfulness, and has revealed to
him a "fountain open for sin." It has led him in
his ruin, helplessness, poverty, and condemnation
to the cross, and there introduced him to a Saviour all sufficient and willing to repair that ruin,
assist that helplessness, enrich that poverty, and
remove that condemnation. Is it any marvel
that, to such an individual, GOD's revealed truth
should be precious? that he should guard it
vigilantly, and love it ardently?

This leads us to revert to the close and important, yet much forgotten connexion which exists
between a clear, spiritual perception of GOD's
truth, and a holy, humble, and close walk with
GOD. The two can never be separated. A
distant and careless walk not only veils the mind
to the glory of the truth, but hardens the heart
to the *power* of the truth. The world in the
heart, guilt upon the conscience, and unmortified

sin in the life, have a fearful and certain tendency
to petrify the moral sensibilities, and render
powerless the sword of the Spirit. Let not
such a professor of Christ wonder that, appeals
the most thrilling, truths the most solemn, and
motives the most persuasive, all, all are disarmed
of their force in his case. Let him not be amazed
that, with an enlightened judgment, and a well
poised creed, and a spotless orthodoxy, he knows
nothing of the holy spiritual actings of the life
of God in the soul, and that he does but hang
a lifeless, sapless, withered branch upon the
Vine, ready to be removed at the Husbandman's
bidding. Let him not be astonished that there
is no close and fervid fellowship with the Father
and His dear Son Christ Jesus,—that his prayers are cold and formal, his conversation vapid
and unedifying, the habitual frame of his mind
earthly and sensual—and that all taste and
desire for the " communion of saints," and for a
spiritual, searching ministry, should have become
extinct in his soul—this is no marvel. The
greater wonder would be if it were otherwise ;
—that if, while living in a state of distance from
God, the ordinances neglected—and sin un-

mortified, the Father and the Son should yet
draw nigh and manifest themselves and so make
known that secret which peculiarly belongs to
those that fear Him.   O how awful is the state
of such a professor !  Does the eye of such an
one scan this page ? let him be affectionately and
earnestly entreated to abandon as worthless his
notional, lifeless religion, humble himself before
the Lord God, implore His forgiveness, and
recover if he has lost, or seek if he never possessed, a sense of acceptance in Christ and
adoption into God's family.   O might we rouse
you to the importance of this ! What consolation
and support will be derived from a formal profession in the hour of death ? What will it avail
after death, when comes the judgment ?   " I
never knew you," will be the withering repulse
of the Saviour.  Be assured, beloved reader, it is
an awful event to die.   To pass onward and
upward to the fearful scrutiny, bearing in the
hand the empty lamp, the outward garb—the name,
the vesture, all, save the *reality* of a justified soul.
To have outwardly professed Christ,—what is
easier ?  To speak respectfully of Him ; to bow
the head at the mention of His name ; to have

assented to His doctrines, and ably and successfully defended His institutions,—nothing less
difficult.   It costs a man nothing to do all this.
There is no cross in it,—and what is a man's
religion if he extract from it the cross ?—there
is no love to Christ influencing, impelling the
soul, and what value are all inferior motives?
there is no singleness of eye to GOD's glory, and
what if *self* only be the idol which the heart sets
up, and before which it burns its daily incense?
But O to have Christ in the heart! This, this is
the truth of God experienced.  Call you it
enthusiasm? Blessed enthusiasm! We exult in
it, we glory in it.   Let the formalist, let the man
of notional religion, let the mere professor call
it what he may, deride it as he will, we admire
the grace, and adore the love, and extol the
power which has formed " Christ within us the
hope of glory." Reader, be satisfied, take
nothing for granted, short of this.

In proportion then to a believer's simple, filial
and close walk with GOD, will be his deep and
spiritual discoveries of truth.   " If any man will
do His will," says Christ, " he shall know of the
doctrine whether it be of GOD."   The more

4*

steadily he walks in GOD's light, the clearer
will he see the light. The nearer he lives to
the Sun of Righteousness the more entirely will
he be flooded with its glory, and the more
vividly will he reflect its brightness. The
more simple and entirely the believing soul
lives on Christ, the more enlarged, experimental
and practical will be his ideas of all truth. The
central fact of the Bible is *Christ crucified.*
From this, as their centre, all the lines of truth
diverge, and to this, as by a common attraction,
they all again return. To know Christ then—
to know Him as dwelling in the heart by His
own Spirit—is to have traversed the great circle
of spiritual truth. What is His own testimony?
" He that hath seen me, hath seen the Father."
'I am the Father's great revelation. I have come
to make Him known. To unveil His attributes,
illustrate His law, to pour forth the ocean fulness
of His love, and to erect one common platform
on which may meet in holy fellowship, GOD
and the sinner,—the two extremes of being.
learn of me, I am the way, the truth, and the
life.'

Not only will a spiritual perception of the

beauty and fitness of the truth be the result of a close and filial intercourse with GOD, but the *assurance* that GOD's Word is *truth* and not fiction, will increase. And to be thoroughly established in this is no small attainment. To know that GOD's Word is *true;* to cherish no doubt or hesitancy ; to give Him full credit for all that He has said—to repose by simple faith upon the promise, and on the faithfulness of Him that has promised, is a blessing earnestly to be sought, and when found, diligently to be kept. A holy walk then will tend much to confirm the soul in the belief of the truth. To quote again the striking words of the Apostle, " he that believeth hath the witness in himself." He has the inward witness to the truth. He needs no outward demonstration. He is in possession of a source of evidence to the truth of God's word which scepticism cannot shake, because it cannot reach it. He may not be able to define the precise nature of his evidence —his reply to the unbelieving objector is, ' it must be *felt* to be known, it must be *experienced* to be understood. This evidence is not the the result of a laboured process of thought. I

arrived not at it by mathematical investigation.
I was convinced by the Eternal Spirit of sin,
fled to Christ, ventured my all upon Him, and
now I know of a surety that GOD's blessed word
*is truth.*' And not more completely was his
sophistry confuted, who attempted to disprove
the doctrine of motion by his opponent immediately rising and walking, than a humble,
spiritual, though unlettered believer, may thus
put to silence the foolishness and ignorance of
men.   Their sophistry he may not be able to
detect, their assertions he may not be able to
disprove, yet by a walk holy and close with
GOD, he may demonstrate to the unbelieving
universe that Jehovah's word is true.   There is
much wisdom in the observation of Coleridge,—
" Evidence of Christianity ! I am weary of the
word ! Make a man feel the want of it ; rouse
him to the self-knowledge of his need of it, and
you may safely trust it to its own evidence."

The truth dear reader, you are now invited
to consider, is, of all truth, the most spiritual and
important.   It is the central fact of the gospel—
its sun, its glory ; yea its very substance ; for
take from it the Atonement and what of the

Gospel remains? It lies at the very basis of a believing sinner's hope. Remove this, and all is gone! Seal up the fountain of Christ's precious blood, and you seal up the soul to blackness, darkness, and despair! And yet in this all important light, how few view it, even of the many who profess a sacred regard for God's Word. The truth of revelation is admitted, and even the necessity of the Atonement, as an essential pillar of immortal hope, is conceded, and still it is but an occasional and transient thought that is conferred upon a subject of the deepest moment and transcendent interest. O that men should treat this subject so! That Jehovah should tabernacle in flesh, and in His humiliation pour out His precious blood as an offering for sin, and that yet we should pass it by with indifference and neglect;—what language is sufficient to describe the affecting spectacle?

# CHAPTER II.

THE ATONEMENT IN ITS RELATION TO THE
GODHEAD OF CHRIST.

**THE DIVINE ATTRIBUTES ENTWINED AROUND THE
TEMPTED AND TREMBLING BELIEVER.**

"The church of GOD which He hath purchased with His own
blood." Acts, xx. 28.

In entering upon the more immediate discussion of this glorious subject, it seems proper
and appropriate that we should begin with the
absolute *Deity of Christ*. The reader will at
once perceive the propriety of this, from a consideration of the single fact, that all the value
and efficacy of the atoning blood, is derived solely
and entirely from the dignity of the person who
sheds it If Christ be not absolutely and truly
what the word of God declares, and what He
Himself professes to be, *the true God*, then as
it regards the great purpose for which His Atonement was made, viz. the satisfaction of Divine

Justice, in a full and entire sacrifice for sin, it were utterly valueless. We feel the vast and solemn importance of this point. We cannot view it lightly, nor discuss it partially. And in reading disquisitions on the Atonement, otherwise able and elaborate, we have been pained to find this single point passed by, with so superficial and casual an allusion. Whereas, it is of the deepest moment. It is the key stone of the arch, sustaining and holding together every part of the mighty fabric. Our examination of the claims of Christ to proper Deity cannot be too close. We cannot too rigidly scrutinize the truth of His Godhead. Jesus Himself challenges investigation. When personally upon earth, carrying forward the great work of redemption, on all occasions, and by all means, He announced and proved His Diety. Thus was He wont to *declare* it :—"I and my Father are one." "Verily, verily, I say unto you, before Abraham was, I am." "I came forth from the Father, and am come into the world; again, I leave the world, and go to the Father." Thus was He wont to *confirm* it :—"I have greater witness than that of John ; for the works which the Father hath given me

to finish, the same works that I do, bear witness
of me that the Father hath sent me." " If I do
not the works of my Father, believe me not.
But if I do, though ye believe not me, believe
the works : that ye may know and believe that
the Father is in me, and I in him." Our blessed
Lord saw and felt the importance of a full belief
in the doctrine of His Godhead. If the foundation of our faith were not laid deep and broad
in this, He well knew that no structure, however
splendid in its external form, could survive the
storm that will eventually sweep away every
lying refuge. And what, to the believing soul,
is more animating than the full unwavering conviction of the fact, that He who bore our sins
in his own body on the tree, was GOD in our
nature. That He who became our surety and
substitute, was JEHOVAH Himself; " God manifest in the flesh." That as GOD, He became
incarnate,—as GOD, He obeyed, and as GOD,
He suffered the penalty. What deep views
does this fact give of sin! what exalted views of
sin's Atonement! Pray, dear reader, that the
blessed and Eternal Spirit may build you up in
the belief of this truth. It is a truth on which

we can live, and on no other truth can we die.
That Satan should often suggest suspicions to
the mind respecting the veracity of this doctrine
we can easily imagine.  That a dear saint of
God should at times find his faith wavering in its
attempts to grasp this wondrous fact, the "incarnate mystery," we marvel not.  It is the very basis
of his hope; is it surprising that Satan should
strive to overturn it?  It is the very sun of the
Christian system; is it surprising that he should
seek to veil it?  Satan's great controversy is with
Christ.   Christ came to overthrow his kingdom,
and He did overthrow it.  Christ came to vanquish
him, and He triumphed.  This signal and total
defeat Satan will never forget.  To regain his kingdom he cannot.   To recover what he has lost he
knows to be impossible.  Therefore his shafts
are levelled against Christ's members.  And the
doctrine, to them most essential and precious,—
the doctrine of Christ's Godhead—is the doctrine
most frequently and severely assailed.  Let no
believer sink in despondency under this severe
temptation.  Let him look afresh to the cross,
afresh to the atoning blood, and faith in Him,
whose word stilled the angry waves of the Gal-
lilean lake, and whose look prostrated to the

5

ground the soldiers sent to His arrest, will give him the victory.

It is our design in this chapter to bring before the reader, in a limited compass, the scripture testimony to the Deity of our adorable Immanuel, and the just inference which is derived in favour of the divine efficacy of His atoning blood. The result of this scripture investigation will compel us to adopt one of two conclusions: —Either that Christ is an imposter—His atonement of no value, and the worship we have rendered Him, mistaken and idolatrous, *or*, that He is all that the scriptures declare Him to be, the supreme God; his death vicarious—and He Himself a just object of spiritual worship. While, if the former conclusion be the one fairly deducible from the Word of God, then it will appear that they who reject Christ's Deity, are opposed to the most stupendous and transcendent display which has, or will ever be made, of the Divine wisdom and goodness, and consequently, dying in this rejection, are doomed to the fearful punishment of those who are found *fighting against God*.

The supreme Deity of Christ rests for its proof

upon the testimony of God's Word. We bring
the doctrine to no other test.  Nor shall we in
examining this testimony perplex the mind of
the reader with needless criticisms.  It is an
erroneous impression which many have imbibed,
that the scriptures cannot be understood without
the constant application of philological criticism,
to bring to light its deep and concealed meaning.
If this were so, then is God's Word lost to more
than two thirds of the human race, who have no
such key to its concealed treasures, and consequently the very purpose of revelation must be
entirely frustrated.  The holy men who wrote
the scripture, under the inspiration of the Holy
Ghost, were in general, plain and unlettered men.
They were educated at the Saviour's feet; and
therefore a beautiful simplicity of style—a style
unadorned by the arts of rhetoric, and untram-
meled by the technicalities of the schools,—
pervades all their writings.  We are far from un-
dervaluing the aid afforded in the investigation
of revealed truth by the labours of able and
learned biblicists—the Church owes them, and
will ever owe them, a debt of gratitude.  "I deny
not the utility of such learning," are the senti-

ments of a profound scholar, and eminent divine,
"but I wish to establish a correct idea of the nature and extent of its utility, as seldom reaching
beyond the explaining of allusions and phrases
of *minor* importance; while the great facts and
doctrines, the precepts and the promises of the
gospel, are expressed in terms the most plain and
the least associated with remote allusions."*
And when we turn our eyes towards Germany,
and discover a decrease in evangelical piety, of
true vital Christianity, almost in the same ratio
with the advance of philological learning, we are
compelled to yield our preference to the scriptural and simple method of investigating religious
truth, viz. "Comparing spiritual things with
spiritual." Jesus Christ is the true GOD. If
this be scripturally proved, then the *inference*
will be indisputable, that His precious blood is
of priceless value, and sovereign efficacy.

It has been usual, in establishing this doctrine,
to refer to the various modes by which GOD has
manifested Himself in His own sacred Word,
and then to trace the application of each and all
these several particulars both in nature and degree

* Dr. Pye Smith.

as they are attributed to the Lord Jesus Christ. The modes of manifestation are;—the *names* which are given to Him—the *attributes* which are ascribed to Him—the *actions* peculiar to Himself—the *relations* which He sustains to created beings—and the *worship* which He has demanded from His intelligent creatures. Let us then proceed to show how Christ stands forth invested with each and all of these several properties of Deity. We begin with the NAMES which are given to God.

The idea conveyed to the mind by the *names* JEHOVAH, LORD, GOD, are self-existence—Omnipotence—Infinite and absolute perfection; indeed they include all the awful attributes which belong to the Divine nature. Now then our argument is this, *Jehovah* is the incommunicable name of the Eternal self-existent GOD—if it can be shown that in the scriptures of truth Christ is called JEHOVAH, LORD, GOD, then Christ is GOD.

We commence with Numbers, xxi. 5, 6, 7. "The people spake against Jehovah, and Jehovah sent fiery serpents among the people, and they bit the people, and much people of Israel

5*

died." Now compare this passage with 1 Cor.
x. 9. "Neither let us tempt Christ as some of
them also tempted, and were destroyed of serpents." To what conclusion do these passages
conduct us, but to the blessed one, that the Person whom the rebellious Israelites tempted, who
inflicted the punishment, and who swore they
should not enter into His rest, was the Eternal
Son of GOD—JEHOVAH Jesus.

Again, Isaiah, vi. 1—6. "In the year that
king Uzziah died I saw also Jehovah sitting
upon a throne, high and lifted up, and his train
filled the temple. Above it stood the seraphims;
each one had six wings; with twain he covered
his face, and with twain he covered his feet, and
with twain he did fly: and one cried unto
another, and said, Holy! Holy! Holy! is Jehovah of hosts! the whole earth is full of his
glory. And the posts of the door moved at the
voice of him that cried, and the whole house
was filled with smoke. Then said I, woe is me,
for I am undone, because I am a man of unclean
lips, and I dwell in the midst of a people of unclean lips: for mine eyes have seen the king
Jehovah of hosts." And in the eighth verse,

"Also I heard the voice of Jehovah, saying, whom shall I send, and who will go for us? Then said I, Here am I, send me! And He said, Go and tell this people, hear ye indeed, but understand not; and see ye indeed, but perceive not; make the heart of this people fat, and make their ears heavy, and shut their eyes, lest they see with their eyes, and hear with their ears, and understand with their heart, and convert and be healed." Compare these passages with John, xii. 39—41. " Therefore they could not believe because that Esaias said again, He hath blinded their eyes and hardened their hearts, that they should not see with their eyes, nor understand with their heart and be converted, and I should heal them. *These things said Esaias, when he saw His glory and spake of Him.*" Whose glory was it that Esaias saw, and of whom did He speak? It was the glory of the only begotten Son of GOD—and of Him He spoke. It was THE GLORY OF CHRIST as the king Jehovah of hosts—The ancient of days, He that was to come. Here, dear reader, might we pause and adore the great Jehovah for this glorious revelation of Himself. Blessed Immanuel! give us, by the teachings of thy Spirit, clear, close, humbling views of thine exalted person. Keep our souls fast anchored on this truth, that thou art God in our nature!

But let us proceed. Regard the declaration of the Evangelist John, i. 1. "In the beginning was the Word, and the Word was with God, and the Word was God." What can more clearly and conclusively prove the real Deity of our dear Lord than these words of the Holy Ghost? Not merely is it declared that the Word was God,—even this would have been overwhelmingly conclusive—but the Word, as distinguished from the Father, and as so distinguished, declared to be God as absolutely as the Father Himself was declared to be God. Another instance in which the term God is applied to Christ, is found in Rom. ix. 5. "Of whom as concerning the flesh Christ came, who is over all, God blessed for ever, Amen." Here is a distinct declaration of the complex person of our Lord. Touching His *humanity*, He came from the Jews; touching His *Deity*, He is God over all. Can language be more explicit? 1 Tim. i 16. "Without controversy, great is the myste of godliness : GOD was manifest in the flesh, justified in the Spirit ; seen of angels, preached unto the Gentiles, believed on in the world, received up into glory." Here Christ is declared to be the *visible* JEHOVAH. GOD embodied in Christ, clear, tangible to our apprehensions. Will not this single passage suffice to remove every doubt ? We have yet other and equally conclusive evidence. Is Jehovah the *great God ? so is Christ ;*—Tit. ii. 13. "Looking for that blessed hope, and the glorious appearing of the *great God* and our Saviour ("the great GOD our Saviour." *marg.*) Jesus Christ." Is Jehovah the *true God ? so is Christ ;*—1 John. v. 20. "We know that the Son of GOD is come and hath given us an understanding that we may know Him that is true : and we are in Him that is true, even in His Son Jesus Christ. *This is the true God*, and eternal life." Is Jehovah the *mighty God ? so is Christ ;*—Isa. ix. 6. " Unto us a child is born, unto us a son is given, and the government shall be upon His shoulder : and His name shall be called Wonderful, Counseller, *The Mighty God*, the Everlasting Father, the Prince of Peace." What was the declaration of

Thomas, after his doubts had vanished, and his mind received the full conviction of the truth? "My Lord and my God!" Again, 2 Peter, i. 1. "Simon Peter, a servant and an apostle of Jesus Christ, to them that have obtained like precious faith with us, through the righteousness of GOD and our Saviour ("God our Saviour," *marg.*) Jesus Christ." 2 Cor. v. 19. "GOD was in Christ, reconciling the world unto Himself," &c. 2 Cor. v. 20. "We are ambassadors for Christ, as though *God did beseech* you by us: we pray you in Christ's stead, be ye reconciled to God;" —in which passage the interchanging of the names GOD and Christ, proves that the *same person* is entitled to both.

Again, let us compare the Word of God with itself. Isa. viii. 13, 14. "Sanctify the Lord of hosts Himself, and let Him be your fear, and let Him be your dread. And He shall be for a sanctuary; but for a stone of stumbling, and for a rock of offence to both houses of Israel." The stone of stumbling and rock of offence, mark, is *the Lord of hosts Himself.* But this stone of stumbling and rock of offence, as appears from the language of Peter, is no other than Christ.

1 Peter, ii. 6. "Wherefore also it is contained in the scripture, Behold I lay in Zion a chief corner stone, elect, precious; and he that believeth in Him shall not be confounded. Unto you, therefore, which believe, He is precious; but unto them which be disobedient, the stone which the builders disallowed, the same is made the head of the corner, and a stone of stumbling, and a rock of offence." Who with a mind not steeled against the truth, but open to conviction, can doubt that, the same Being who is called Jehovah of hosts in the Old Testament, is the Lord Jesus Christ in the New. To the proud and unbelieving Jews, He was a stone of stumbling, and rock of offence, but to us who believe, He is precious.

Further. Isa. xliv. 6. "Thus saith the Lord the king of Israel and His redeemer the Lord of hosts, I am the first, and I am the last, and besides me there is no God." Compare with Rev. xxii. 13. "I (Jesus) am Alpha and Omega, the beginning and the end, the first and the last." These titles are confined to Him alone, besides whom there is no GOD. Jesus has assumed these titles to Himself; the inference, strictly

logical, is,—*Jesus is* GOD. We would also direct
the reader to that remarkable prophecy which
was fully accomplished in Christ, recorded by
Zech. xi. 12. "If ye think good, give me my
price; and if not forbear: so they weighed for
my price thirty pieces of silver. And the Lord
said unto me, Cast it unto the potter, a goodly
price that I was prized at of them. And I took
the thirty pieces of silver, and cast them to the
potter in the house of the Lord."—Who is the
speaker in this passage? JEHOVAH. Who was
sold? JEHOVAH JESUS. At what price? for thirty
pieces of silver. Let the reader turn for the
exact fulfilment of this prophecy, to Matt. xxvii.
3—10. "Then Judas which had betrayed Him,
when he saw that he was condemned, repented
himself, and brought again the thirty pieces of
silver to the chief priest and elders, saying, I
have sinned, in that I have betrayed the innocent
blood. And they said, what is that to us? see
thou to that. And he cast down the pieces of silver
in the temple, and departed and went and hanged
himself. And the chief priests took the silver
pieces, and said, It is not lawful for to put them
in the treasury, because it is the price of blood.

and they took counsel and bought with them the
otter's field, to bury strangers in. Wherefore
lat field was called the field of blood, unto this
ay. Then was fulfilled that which was spoken
y Jeremy (or Zechariah*) the prophet, saying,
and they took the thirty pieces of silver, the
rice of Him that was valued, whom they of the
hildren of Israel did value : and gave them for
le potters field, as the Lord appointed me."
'he last proof we quote is Isa. xlv. 23. "I have
worn by myself, the word is gone out of my
louth in righteousness, and shall not return, that
nto me every knee shall bow, every tongue
hall swear." Compare this prophecy with
lom. xiv. 11, the apostle argues that all creation
hould do honour to Christ, "for it is written,

* "The words here quoted are not found in *Jeremiah*, but in
*echariah ;* and a variety of conjectures have been formed in order
reconcile this discrepancy. The most probable opinion seems to
, that the name of the prophet was originally omitted by the Evan-
list, and that the name of *Jeremiah* was added by some subsequent
pyist. It is omitted in the two M.S.S. of the twelfth century, in the
rriac, later Persic, two of the Itala, and in some other Latin copies ;
id what renders it highly probable that the original reading was dia
u prophetai, *by the prophet*, is, that Matthew frequently omits the
ime of the prophet in his quotations—See Ch. i. 22.—ii. 5, 15.—
ii. 35.—xxi. 4. This omission is approved of by Bengel, Dr. A.
arke, and Horne."—*Bag. Comp. Bib. note.*

As I live saith the Lord, every knee shall bow to me, and every tongue shall confess to God." What is the solemn inference ?—that the GOD who predicates that all men shall give account to Him and stand before Him, is the same referred to in the tenth verse—"we shall all stand before the judgment seat of *Christ.*" Thus have we shown from the simple testimony of scripture, that Christ is without qualification or diminution, JEHOVAH, LORD, GOD. We now proceed to show that the Lord Jesus, our adorable Immanuel, is represented in GOD's word as invested with all the ATTRIBUTES which belong to Jehovah.

Let us commence with His ETERNAL EXISTENCE. If it can be proved from the sacred Scriptures that this belongs to Christ, it must follow that He is GOD ; for of no other being can it be said that He is *eternal* but Jehovah. Examine then Coloss. i. 17, 18. "And He is before all things, and by Him all things consist. And He is the head of the body, the church, who is the beginning, the first born from the dead ; that in all things he might have the preeminence." In this striking and beautiful passage Jesus is declared to be before all created things; could this be true, if He *Himself* were a created being? Christ is either created or He is uncreated. He is a creature or the Creator. There is no intermediate scale of being. We repeat it, He must be one of two, the creature or the Creator. If a mere creature—and the Socinian allows Him to be no more—then it were an absurdity to suppose him creating all things, for he must have been created before He could create, then He could not have been *before* all created things. If too, He were a mere creature,—and still let it be remembered the Socinian and Arian deny that He is more—how could he uphold all things? For He would need an upholding power for Himself. No mere creature ever has or ever can sustain itself. The angels could not, for they fell. Adam could not, for he fell. And Christ could not have sustained Himself in the solemn hour of Atonement, when standing beneath the mighty load of His people's sins, had He not been more than creature—the uncreated Jehovah. His humanity did indeed tremble and shudder and shrink back—but upborne by his Godhead,— secretly, invisibly, yet effectually sustained by his Deity, He achieved a complete triumph, made an end of sin, and brought in a new and everlasting righteousness. If, too, he were a creature only, how could He give spiritual life to the dead, and how could He sustain that life when given? All spiritual life is from Christ, and all spiritual life is sustained by Christ. " Christ who is our life,"—the life of the soul —the life of pardon, the life of justification, the life of sanctification, the life of all the Christian graces; the life of all that now is, and the life of all that is to come. Glorious truth this, to the saint of GOD!

Compare Rev. i. 8. " I am Alpha and Omega, the beginning and the ending, saith the Lord, which is, and which was, and which is to come, the Almighty." Isa. xliv. 6. " Thus saith the Lord the King of Israel, and His Redeemer the Lord of Hosts, I am the first and I am the last and besides me there is no God." We refra: from commenting on these passages, so se evident is the truth. Turn to our blessed Lor conference with the Jews, in which He asse His Eternal existence. John, viii. 58. " Je said unto them, Verily, verily, I say unto :

before Abraham was, I am." Does not Jehovah
apply these very terms to Himself? Exod. iii.
14. " And God said unto Moses, I am that I
am." How then are we to understand these
words? Not by the Socinian's gloss, but by the
conduct of the Jews, " Then took they up stones
to cast at Him." They considered Christ guilty
of blasphemy, in applying to Himself the incommunicable name and attributes of Jehovah. They
perfectly understood Him to mean that he was
God. Had he not been truly Divine, would He
have left them under so fearful a delusion? And
would He have jeopardized His life, when by a
single retraction He could have allayed their
rage, and averted the danger that threatened
Him? What a consoling view do we derive
of Christ, from this revealed attribute of his
nature. Is He *eternal?* then His love to His
people is eternal; His love to them being coeval
with his very being. It is not the love of yesterday or of to-day,—it is the love of *eternity.*
Its spring-head is His own eternal existence.
Is he *eternal?* then must He be *unchangeable*
too. His precious love set upon them from all
eternity, can never be removed. Having given

6*

them Himself, Himself He will never take
away. Blessed thought ! He may blight earthly
hopes ; He may break up earthly cisterns ; He
may wither earthly gourds—He may send billow
upon billow, breach upon breach, but never, never
will he take Himself from the people of His love.
Dear reader, you may be conscious of many
and great departures.   This single view of your
Father's unchangeableness, may recall to your
recollection backslidings many and aggravated.
Forgetfulness, ingratitude, unkindnesses without
number ; murmurings, rebellion, and unbelief.
Still does GOD, your GOD, say to you 'though
thou hast dealt so with me, though thou hast
forgotten me, though thy name is rebellious, yet
do I love thee still.   Return unto me, and I will
return unto you.'   What a soul-humbling, heart-
melting thought is this !   Does your Father love
your sins ? Nay—does He look complacently on
your wanderings ? Nay ! He hates your sins
and He will follow your wanderings with Hi
chastising rod ; but He loves your perso
beholding you in the Beloved, fully and free
accepted in the glorious righteousness of Jes
who is the same "yesterday, to-day, and foreve

If this truth, dear reader, be broken up to your soul by the blessed and eternal Spirit, the effect will be most holy and abasing. The legitimate tendency of all spiritual truth is sanctifying. Hence our blessed Lord prayed that the *truth* might be the medium through which His people should be sanctified. "Sanctify them *through the truth*." John, xvii. 17. "And for their sakes I sanctify myself, that they also might be *sanctified through the truth*." Ver. 19. And hence the apostle reasons, "Christ also loved the church and gave Himself for it: That He might sanctify and cleanse it with the washing of water, *by the word*." Eph. v. 26. That GOD's truth has been, and is abused by wicked and ungodly men, is no argument against the truth. They abuse it to their own condemnation. They turn it from its right and legitimate use to their own loss. Still, the truth stands erect in its peerless dignity and holy tendency. And when unfolded to the understanding, and laid upon the heart by the Holy Spirit, Christ's prayer is answered, in the progressive sanctification of the soul.

OMNIPRESENCE is an attribute of Deity ascribed to Christ. We would refer the reader to

two portions of scripture for proof; they both
run in parallel lines with each other. In Matt.
xviii, 20, we have this encouraging declaration
from Christ, "Where two or three are gathered
together in my name, there am I in the midst of
them." Compare this with Exod. xx. 24. "In
all places where I record my name, I will come
unto thee and will bless thee." Thus the reader
will perceive that the identical promise which
GOD gave to His ancient church, when He established her in the wilderness, when He gave
to her the law, built for her the tabernacle, and
instituted for her a sacrifice the Lord Jesus
makes of Himself. Consoling thought! Jesus
is with His saints at all times, in all places, and
under all circumstances. He is "God with us."
He is with them to comfort them in the hour of
sorrow, to enlighten them in the hour of darkness, to guide them in the hour of doubt and
perplexity, to deliver them in the time of con-
flict, to support them in the hour of death. O for
faith to realize this! He was with His three
faithful servants in the fiery furnace; He was
with Daniel in the lion's den; He was with
Jacob in his wrestlings at Bethel; He was with

John in his exile at Patmos. Jesus is at all
times, in all places, and under all circumstances
with His dear people. Reader are you a child
of sorrow? Perhaps you are a son or a daughter
of affliction. You may now be passing through
the furnace ;—You may now be draining adversity's bitter cup. The rod of the covenant may
be heavy upon you. Friends unkind, the world
empty, every thing earthly changing, faith weak,
corruptions strong, and what embitters the cup,
and deepens the shade, your Father hiding from
you his dear reconciled face. Is it so? Still is
your omnipresent Jesus with you. Be not cast
down. This furnace is but to consume the tin
and burnish the gold. This draught is but to
work your inward good. These painful dispensations, by which you are learning the change-
ableness of every thing earthly, are but to wean
you from a poor, unsatisfying world, and to draw
you near and yet nearer to Jesus. Then be of
good cheer, for he hath promised never to leave
or forsake you. So that you may boldly say,
"the Lord is my helper."

Regard the attribute of OMNISCIENCE as belonging essentially to Christ. John. ii. 24, 25.

"But Jesus did not commit Himself unto them, because He knew all men, and needed not that any should testify of man: for He knew what was in man." We beseech the reader to regard attentively the 1 Kings, viii. 39, where the same attribute, in almost the same expressions, is ascribed to Jehovah. "For thou, EVEN THOU ONLY knowest the hearts of all the children of men." Whose prerogative is it to search the heart? who can fathom this fathomless sea of iniquity? who can follow it in all its serpentine windings? who can detect its deep subtilty? Who? "I the Lord search the heart, I try the reins." A mere creature—such as the denier of Christ's proper Deity would make Him—cannot know the heart. It is a perfection peculiar to GOD and must in its own nature be incommunicable; for were it communicable to a creature it could not be peculiar to GOD Himself. Were it possible we say, that GOD should delegate the power and prerogative of searching the heart and trying the reins of the children of men to a mere created being, then it could with no propriety be said of Him that *He only* searcheth the heart. *And yet to Jesus does this attribute belong.* In

the prophecy of Jeremiah, xviii. 10, the Lord
says, "I Jehovah search the heart and try the
reins, to give every man according to His ways."
In Rev. ii. 23, Christ says,—and He would
have it proclaimed through the churches as the
true doctrine of the gospel—"And all the churches
shall know that I am He who searcheth the
reins and hearts, and I will give unto every one
of you according unto your works." Is not then
the evidence of His Deity most conclusive?
Who can resist it? From this attribute of Christ
what blessedness flows to the believing soul?
It is at all times a consolation to him to remember that Jesus knows and searches the heart.
His iniquity He sees and subdues; for the promise is, "He will subdue our iniquities." Mich.
vii. 19. He detects some lurking evil, some la-
tent corruption, and before it develops itself in
the outward departure, the overt act, He checks
and conquers it. 'Cheering thought,' may the
believer say, 'that all my inbred evil, the hidden
corruption of my heart is known to my Saviour
God. Lord I would not hide it from thee. I
would not veil from thine eye a single corruption.
I *would not conceal* a thought, but would cry,

"search me, O God, and know my heart, try me,
and know my thoughts; and see if there be any
wicked way in me, and lead me in the way
everlasting.'" Ps. cxxxix. 23, 24. He sees too,
*His own gracious work in the soul.* The little
spiritual life that He has breathed there—the
little grace that He has implanted there—the
little spark of love that He has kindled there
—the faint and feeble longings after Him—the
inward strugglings with sin—the hungering and
thirsting for holiness—the panting for Divine
conformity—all is known to Jesus. The Lord
Jesus knows and recognises His own work.
The counterfeit He soon detects. The outward
garb and the unhumbled spirit—the external
profession and the unbroken heart, escape not
His piercing glance. Man may be deceived,
the Lord Jesus never. We may not be able to
discern between the righteous and the wicked—
between nature and grace—between the outward
profession and the inward reality, but Jesus
knows what is genuine and what is base—what
is the work of His own blessed Spirit, and what
is the mere effect of an enlightened judgment,
*and an alarmed* conscience. Dear reader, this

is His own solemn declaration of Himself—"I
the Lord search the heart." Can you open all
your heart to Him? Can you admit Him within
its most secret places? Are you willing to have
no concealments. Are you willing that He
should search and prove it? O be honest with
God! keep nothing back—tell Him all that you
detect within you. He loves the full, honest
disclosure. He delights in this confiding surrender of the whole heart. Are you honest in
your desires that He might sanctify your heart,
and subdue all its iniquity? then confess all to
Him;—tell Him all. You would not conceal
from your physician a single symptom of your
disease. You would not hide any part of the
wound—but you would, if anxious for a complete
cure, disclose to him all. Be you as honest
with the Great Physician—the Physician of your
soul. It is true He knows your case—it is true
He anticipates every want, yet He will have,
and delights in having, His child approach Him
with a full and honest disclosure. Let David's
example encourage you: " I acknowledged my
sin unto thee, and mine iniquity have I not hid:
I said I will confess my transgressions unto the

7

Lord ; and thou forgavest the iniquity of my sin.*
Ps. xxxi. 5. And while the heart is thus pouring
itself out in a full and minute confession, let the
eye of faith be fixed on Christ. It is only in
this posture that the soul shall be keep from despondency. Faith must rest itself upon the atoning blood. And O, in this posture, fully and
freely, beloved reader, may you pour out your
heart to God! Disclosures you dare not make
to your tenderest friend, you may make to Him.
Sins you would not confess, corruption you
would not acknowledge as existing within you,
you are privileged, thus "looking unto Jesus,"
to pour into the ear of your Father and God.
And O, how the heart will become unburthened,
and the conscience purified, and peace and joy
flow into the soul by this opening of the heart
to God. Try it, dear reader. Let no consciousness of guilt keep you back. Let no unbelieving suggestion of Satan, that such confessions are
inappropriate for the ear of God restrain you.
Come at once—come *now*—rush to your Father's
feet, and bringing in your hands the precious
blood of Christ, make a full and free disclosure.
*Thus from* the attribute of Christ's Omniscience,

may a humble believer extract much consolation—at all times permitted to appeal to it, and say with Peter, "Lord thou knowest all things, thou knowest that I love thee."

OMNIPOTENCE is declared to belong to Jesus. Compare Ps. xlv. 3. "Gird thy sword upon thy thigh, O most mighty." Rev. i. 8. I am Alpha and Omega, the beginning and the ending, saith the Lord, which is and which was, and which is to come, THE ALMIGHTY." Compare Ver. 6, 7, of the same Psalms, "Thy throne, O GOD, is forever and ever: the sceptre of thy kingdom is a right sceptre. Thou lovest right-eousness and hatest wickedness : therefore GOD thy GOD, hath anointed thee with the oil of glad-ness above thy fellows." Heb. i. 8, 9, where the same words are quoted and applied to Christ. And let us glance at the authoritative manner with which He executes His mighty acts of grace. Mark his deportment. Was there ought that betrayed the consciousness of an inferior, the submission of a dependant, the weakness of a mortal, or the imperfection of a sinner ? Did not the GOD shine through the man with majes-tic awe, when to the lepers He said, "I will, be thou clean." To the man with the withered hand, "Stretch forth thy hand"——To the blind, "receive thy sight"—To the dead, "I say unto thee, arise." And to the tumultuous waves, "peace, be still." Dear reader, are you an experimental believer in Jesus? then this Omnipotent Christ is wedded to your best interests. He is Omnipotent to save—Omnipotent to protect—Omnipotent to deliver—Omnipotent to subdue all your iniquities, to make you humble, holy and obedient. All power resides in Him. "It pleased the Father that in Him"—in Him as the Mediator of His church—"all fulness should dwell." Not a corruption, but He is omnipotent to subdue it—not a temptation, but He is omnipotent to overcome it—not a foe, but He is omnipotent to conquer it—not a fear but He is omnipotent to quell it. "All power," is His own consoling language, "all power is given unto me in heaven and in earth." Could any mere creature assert this of himself? Never, without the deepest blasphemy, "Cry out and shout, O inhabitant of Zion, for great is the Holy One of Israel in the midst of thee." From this view of the Divine attributes, *let us pass* to a consideration of the DIVINE works attributed to Christ, and such as no mere creature could perform.

The work of CREATION belongs to Him. Col. i. 16. 17. " By·Him were all things created that are in heaven and that are in earth, visible and invisible; whether they be thrones or dominions, or principalities or powers, all things were created by Him and for Him.  And He is before all things, and by Him all things consist." If then He be the creator, He must be GOD.  The glory of creation is given to Him by the redeemed in heaven. " They cast their crowns before the throne, saying, thou art worthy, O Lord to receive glory and honour and power, for thou hast created all things, and for thy pleasure they are and were created." Rev. iv. 2. What a thought is this——that the great Creator of all things once trod, in human form, the world of His own creating——for " He was in the world, and the world was made by Him, and the world knew Him not." John, i. 10. And so is He the author of the new spiritual creation.  He spake and there was life, light, and order in the soul, where before there was death, darkness and derangement,

7*

Let us give Him the glory of both creations, the natural and the spiritual.

PROVIDENCE is another Divine work as truly belonging to Christ. Thus He says, Matt. xxviii. 18, "All power is given to me in heaven and in earth." "He is Lord of all." Acts, x. 36. "Lord both of the dead and the living." Rom. xiv. 9. "Christ is above all principality and power, might and dominion, and every name that is named, not only in this world, but also in that which is to come." Eph. i. 20—22. "Upholding all things by the word of His power." Heb. i. 2. "By Him (Christ) all things consist." Col. iv. 17. "The Prince of the kings of the earth." Rev. i. 5. Thus is it clear that Jesus is the GOD of providence. The government of all worlds and of all creatures, according to the prediction of prophecy, is upon His shoulders. Is not this thought full of rich comfort and consolation to the experienced believer? Jesus is the GOD of providence. All your steps, dear reader, if you are His, are ordered and directed by Him;—by Him who is GOD in your nature—by Him who loved you unto the death—by Him who is your *Elder Brother*, your Prophet, Priest, and King.

O how tranquilizing to the soul in the hour of its deep sorrow and bereavement, to know that it is sheltered in the hollow of those very hands which were once pierced for us. That Christ has blended with His mediatorial character, His providential government—that the Redeemer who died to save, is the GOD who lives to sway the sceptre. It has been well remarked, that Providence was intended to be the handmaid to Grace, but that Grace only can unfold the steps of Providence. It is only the experimental believer who can clearly discern the movements of an invisible hand in all the affairs and incidents of life. He has learned to acknowledge the Lord in all His ways, and to commit to His disposal all His steps. And He who thus guides and governs is the Mediator—the Christ who obeyed, suffered, and died in our behalf. O consoling thought! Christian reader, ponder this! what are your present circumstances? Are you *persecuted* for Jesus' sake? Listen to His own cheering words,—"Marvel not if the world hate you, for ye know that it hated me before it hated you." "In the world ye shall have tribulation; but *be of good* cheer; I have overcome the

world." Are you in circumstances of *want?*
what does he say; "Take no thought for your
life what ye shall eat, or what ye shall drink;
nor yet for your body what ye shall put on. Is
not the life more than meat, and the body than
raiment? Behold the fowls of the air: for they
sow not, neither do they reap, nor gather into
barns; yet your heavenly Father feedeth them.
Are ye not much better than they." "But seek
ye first the kingdom of God and His righteousness; and all these things shall be added unto
you." Are you perplexed to know the path of
duty?—longing to know the way the Lord would
have you walk?—This is His promise: "Call
upon me in the day of trouble, and I will deliver."
"Commit thy way unto the Lord; trust also in
Him; and He shall bring it to pass." "The
steps of a good man are ordered by the Lord,
and He delighteth in his way." Are you sore
pressed by *temptation?* see how the Holy Ghost
would lead you to the sympathy and tenderness
of Jesus—"He took not on Him the nature of
angels, but He took on Him the seed of Abraham. Wherefore in all things it behoved Him
*to be* made like unto His brethren, that He

might be a merciful and faithful High Priest in
things pertaining to God, to make reconciliation
for the sins of the people.   For in that He Himself hath suffered being tempted, He is able to
succour them that are tempted."   "For we have
not an High Priest which cannot be touched
with the feeling of our infirmities; but was in all
points tempted like as we are, yet without sin.
Let us therefore come boldly unto the throne of
grace, that we may obtain mercy, and find grace
to help in time of need."    Are you oppressed by
present or anticipated *trials*?  Hearken again to
His dear voice:"Let not your hearts be troubled;
ye believe in God, believe also in me." John,
xiv. 1.   Whatever may be the dark and gloomy
aspect of things around you, yet Jesus does all
things well—and all things, however adverse,
and apparently severe, yet *all* things are working
for your present and ultimate good.  ·

The last Divine work belonging to Christ to
which we allude, is that of JUDGING THE WORLD.
This, the most sceptical will acknowledge, peculiarly belongs to God.  In Eccl. xii. 14, we
read, "God shall bring every work into judgment, *with* every secret thing, whether it be

good or whether it be evil."—Now it is most
clear, that *Christ* shall be the Judge. For so
we read—"We must all stand before the judgment seat of *Christ*."—"He shall judge the quick
and the dead at His appearing." &c. "The
Father judgeth no man, but hath committed all
judgment to the Son." John, v. 22. Could this
office be filled, and this power exercised by a
mere creature?—Are not Omnipotence, Omniscience, and Omnipresence indispensably necessary to qualify the Judge of all for the high office?
We have shown that Christ is fully invested
with all these qualifications,—that He is fully
qualified to sit in judgment at His second coming,
upon the beings whom He created. The Redeemer of men then will be the Judge of men.
He who once appeared in the mild and gentle
character of a *Saviour*, will then appear in the
terrific form of a *Judge*. Men will not then
question His Godhead—men will not then dis-
pute His Deity—but "to Him every knee shall
bow, and every tongue confess that He is LORD
to the glory of God the Father." To the believer in Jesus, what a transporting thought' is
this,—that his Saviour shall be his Judge. That

in the face of Him who shall sit upon the great white throne—before Him gathered for judgment all nations, he will recognize a Friend—a Brother —a Redeemer—an Advocate. Dear reader, have *you* an Advocate with the Father? What is *your* foundation in view of that solemn day? A professor of Christ you may be, but is His blood and righteousness at the root of that profession? Are you building as a poor empty comdemned sinner—disclaiming all merit, all self-righteousness, all works—upon a crucified Saviour? What know you of the broken heart—of the contrite spirit? What know you of the precious blood of Christ? O examine yourself, be affectionately entreated, for in the day when Christ shall judge the world in righteousness, all mere outward profession, all notional religion, will wither away, and if you are found destitute of a better righteousness than your own, even the finished righteousness of Christ—how appalling will be the consequences!

We have now arrived at the last source of argument in proof of our Lord's absolute Deity— and that is, the DIVINE WORSHIP which belongs to Him. We feel this to be strong ground. It will

be acknowledged that one end of revelation was to
expel from the world polytheism and idolatry, by
teaching that, GOD, and GOD only, was to receive
the adoration and worship of men.  Now if it can
be shown by a reference to the simple declarations of GOD's Word, that the Lord Jesus received and encouraged the adoration and worship
due only to proper Deity, then most triumphantly
shall we have established this glorious doctrine
of the gospel, that Christ is GOD.  The reader
will bear in mind that solemn command of Jehovah, recorded in Exod. xx. 3. " Thou shalt
have no other gods before me."  Let him then
turn to Heb. i. 6. " And again when He bringeth
in the first begotten into the world, He saith,
And let all the angels of God worship Him."
What can be more conclusive.  Here, in usher-
ing into the world His only begotten Son, the
Father claims for Him the adoration and worship
belonging exclusively to Deity.  Would He have
so contradicted Himself—trampled upon his own
law, had not Christ been coequal with Himself?
Never!  Yet further,—if Christ had been a mere
man, why did He not check those persons who,
when He was on earth, presented to Him Divine

homage? We find that Paul and Barnabas refused the worship that was offered them as Divine. When Cornelius would have worshipped Peter, he said, "Stand up for I myself also am a man." And when John in the Apocalypse, mistook a celestial messenger for a Divine being, and would have worshipped him, the angel immediately abjured the homage, and said, "See thou do it not, for I am of the fellow servants the Apostles * * * * worship God." And yet Jesus refused not, but rather encouraged Divine homage when He tabernacled in the flesh. "Depart from me, for I am a sinful man, O Lord," was the exclamation of Peter when he caught a sudden glimpse of the Godhead of Jesus, reminding us of an equivalent expression of the prophet Isaiah, "Then said I, wo is me, for I am undone, for mine eyes have seen the Lord of hosts." Isa. vi. 5. And what was the last act of the disciples, as they saw the sacred form of their Lord, ascending and lessening from their view?—it was a solemn act of worship—we read that "they worshipped Him, and returned to Jerusalem with great joy." Luke, xxiv. 52.

Having followed us through this mass of

8

scriptural evidence in favour of Christ's proper
Deity, the reader will now be prepared to pass
to the INFERENCE which is fairly deducible from
the doctrine—viz. That the Atonement of Christ
is of *infinite value* and *efficacy*.   Let the remark
already made, be borne in mind, that if Christ
were a mere creature, if he claimed no higher .
dignity than Gabriel, or one of the Prophets or
Apostles, then His atonement, as it regards the
satisfaction of Divine Justice, the honouring of
the Law, the pardon of sin, the peace of the
conscience, and the salvation of the soul, would
possess no intrinsic efficacy whatever.   It would
be but the atonement of a finite being,—a being
possessing no superior merit to these in whose
behalf the atonement was made.   We state it
then broadly and unequivocally, that the entire
glory, dignity, value, and efficacy of Christ's precious blood which He shed for sin, rests entirely
upon the Deity of His person.   If the Deity of
Christ sinks, the atonement of Christ sinks with
it.   If the one stands, so stands the other.   How
strong are the words of Paul addressed to the
Ephesian Elders, "Take heed therefore unto
yourselves, and to all the flock over which the

Holy Ghost hath made you overseers, to feed *the church of God which he hath purchased with His own blood.*" Acts, xx. 28. How conclusive to the question before us is this testimony ! The blood that purchased the church was *Divine*. It was indeed the blood of Christ's humanity—for His human nature alone could suffer, bleed and die—yet deriving all its glory, value and efficacy from the union of the human with the Divine nature. It was the blood of the GOD man, Jehovah Jesus. No inferior blood could have sufficed. The law which Adam, our federal head, broke, before it could release the sinner from its penalty, demanded a sacrifice infinitely holy, and infinitely great. One equal with the Father— the dignity of whose person would impart infinite merit to His work, and the infinite merit of whose work, would fully sustain its honour and its purity. All this was found in the person of Christ. In His complex person He was eminently fitted for the mighty work. As GOD, He obeyed the precepts and maintained the honour of the law ;—*as man*, He bore its curse and endured its penalty. It was the blending as into one, these two natures ;—the bringing together

these extremes of being, the finite and the infinite, which shed such resplendent lustre on
His atonement, which stamped such worth and
efficacy on His blood. No subject discussed in
these pages claims such vast importance as this.
I beseech the reader, treat it not lightly. Deem
it not a useless speculation. It is of the deepest
moment. If the blood of Christ possess not infinite merit, infinite worth, it could never be efficacious in washing away the guilt of sin, or in
removing the dread of condemnation. When
you come to die, this, of all truths, if you are an
experimental believer, will be the most precious
and sustaining. In that solemn hour, when the
curtain that conceals the future parts, and eternity lets down upon the view the full blaze of its
awful realities,—in that hour, when all false de-
pendencies will crumble beneath you, and sin's
long catalogue passes in review before you—O
then to know that, the Saviour on whom you
depend is GOD in your nature—that the blood in
which you have washed has in it all the efficacy
and value of Deity, this, this will be the alone
plank that will buoy up the soul in that awful
moment, and at that fearful crisis. The author

lately saw one die. And his testimony to the sustaining power of Christ's Deity in that moment was given in these words—"If Christ was not my *Creator*, what could I do now?" O precious truth this, for a poor believing soul to rest upon! We wonder not that "he who has Jesus is safe even amid the perils of the sea."* We wonder not that, fast anchored on this truth, amid circumstances the most appalling, death in view, wearing its most terrific aspect, the believer in Jesus can survey the scene with composure, and quietly yield his spirit unto the hands of Him who redeemed it.

* The last words of the Rev. G. Cowles, who with his wife, was lost in the Steampacket "Home," on Cape Hatteras, Nov. 9, 1837.

8*

# CHAPTER III.

## THE SPECIALITY OF THE DESIGN OF THE ATONEMENT.

### THE ENTIRE PARDON AND JUSTIFICATION OF THE BELIEVING SINNER.

"In that day there shall be a fountain opened to the house of David, and to the inhabitants of Jerusalem, for sin and uncleanness." Zech. xiii. 1.

WE have already, in the leading chapter of this work, remarked upon the incompetency of natural reason to understand spiritual truth. Neither the nature, the harmony, or the end of Divine truth can it discern. This incapacity may be traced, not to a deficiency of mental endowment, or to the extreme abstruseness of revelation;—for the weakest intellect, enlightened and sanctified by the Spirit of GOD, may grasp the profoundest doctrine in the great system of theology, so far as the revelation of that doctrine extends

—but, to the want of a spiritually renewed mind. This is the cause, and this only. There is the mind, and there is the truth; the one vigorous, the other lucid; and yet there is no sympathy, the one with the other. How, on other grounds, can it be accounted for? There is no spiritual taste for the investigation of GOD's holy Word. The moral tone of the mind harmonizes not with its holy and lofty themes. The one is on the side of holiness, the other on the side of sin. The one asserts the authority and spirituality of the law, the other assumes the attitude of hostility to that law. Where then is the affinity? where the sympathy? On other subjects it may be at home; here, it is tossed upon an open sea. In the investigation of other themes, it may prove itself a giant in power; here, it betrays the feebleness of a dwarf. It follows then, as a self evident truth, that the mind must be changed, and changed by GOD Himself, before Divine truth will either be understood or received. Hence we find the Apostle, in behalf of the Ephesian Christian's, thus praying: " That the God of our Lord Jesus Christ, the Father of glory may give unto you

the spirit of wisdom and revelation in the knowledge of Him, the eyes of your understanding
being enlightened," &c. Eph. i. 17, 18.

Of all the doctrines of the Gospel, thus dark
and inexplicable to an unrenewed mind, is the
doctrine of Christ's Atonement in its especial
and gracious design. This can only be understood by a mind awakened to the nature and
turpitude of SIN. As the expiation of *sin* was
the great design of Christ's wondrous death, so
no individual, thus ignorant of sin, however vast
his mental powers, and however firm his belief in the truth of Divine revelation, can discover
and welcome this truth. We speak not, and
need we again assure the reader, of mere theo-
retical views of truth. O no! We speak of a
higher grade of knowledge than this. There is
as wide a difference as possibly can be, between
a reception of the truth in the judgment, and the
reception of the truth in the heart. Let no man
be deceived. To deceive others is awful—but
to deceive oneself, more awful yet! It is to this
natural darkness; this ignorance of sin; this
want of the Spirit's teaching, that we are to attribute all the false and erroneous views that

men have advanced touching the nature and design of Christ's death. It is our solemn belief, that all error in theology, especially that which undermines the Atonement, has its rise in the setting aside the law of GOD. Let the law be fully recognized in its Divine authority, its inflexible dignity, and its spotless purity; let its condemnatory sentence be felt in the soul—let all hope of justification by its obedience be swept away, and let the sinner stand forth in the full blaze of its terrors, and then will be seen the absolute *necessity* of an Atonement, and precisely such an Atonement as the adorable Redeemer offered upon the cross. No individual then, taught by the Spirit, who is emphatically designated "The Spirit of *Truth*,"—made to see the exceeding sinfulness of sin as against a holy God—emptied of all self-sufficiency—the eye open to the inward plague, and laid prostrate in the dust as a poor, broken-hearted sinner —no individual thus taught, would ever affirm that Jesus died with any other design than that for which He did die, viz. *to offer to Divine Justice a full and infinite satisfaction for sin.* This brings us to the immediate discussion of the

subject.    May we feel, that the ground on
which we now stand, is holy.    If there be a
subject, the consideration of which we should
approach with caution, humility and prayer, it is
this.    May our hearts be lifted up to GOD for
the teachings of His Spirit, whose blessed office,
in the economy of grace it is, to glorify Christ,
" taking of the things that belong to Him, and
showing them to the soul." John, xvi. 14.    O
for His holy anointing, while we treat of this
stupendous subject; CHRIST PRESENTING HIM-
SELF A SACRIFICE FOR SIN!    For the purpose of
presenting the subject clearly before the mind
of the reader, we shall    first    adduce those
prominent portions of GOD's Word, which declare the end and design of Christ's death to be
an *Atonement for sin;* it will then be appropriate
to show that, the Atonement of Christ is a *full*
and *entire* blotting out of the sins of His people;
this will prepare us to glance at the great covenant *blessings* which an experimental belief of
this truth conveys into the soul.

The Word of GOD, the only rule of faith and
duty, distinctly and invariably represents the
*death of* Jesus as a *sacrifice,* and the especial

and gracious design of that sacrifice, *an Atonement for sin*. If this is denied, how are we to interpret the following remarkable passages :—
'He was wounded for our transgressions, He was bruised for our iniquities: the chastisement of our peace was upon Him, and with His stripes we are healed." Isa. liii. 5. "The Lord laid on Him the iniquity of us all." Ver. 6. "This is my blood of the New Testament which is shed for many, for the remission of sins." Matt. xxvi. 28. "When we were without strength, in due time Christ died for the ungodly." Rom. v. 25. "He hath made Him to be sin, (or a sin-offering,) for us, who knew no sin, that we might be made the righteousness of GOD in Him." 2 Cor. v. 21. "In whom we have redemption through His blood, the forgiveness of sins according to the riches of His grace." Eph. i. 7. 'For as much as ye know, that ye were not redeemed with corruptible things, as silver and gold, from your vain conversation received by tradition from your fathers;' but with the precious blood of Christ, as of a lamb without blemish and without spot." 1 Peter, i. 18, 19. "For f the *blood of bulls* and of goats, and the ashes

of an heifer sprinkling the unclean, sanctifyeth
to the purifying of the flesh; how much more
shall the blood of Christ, who through the Eternal Spirit offered Himself without spot to God,
purge your conscience from dead works to serve
the living God." Heb. ix. 13, 14. "Herein is
love, not that we loved God, but that He loved
us, and sent His Son to be the propitiation for
our sins." 1 John iv. 10. How perfectly unin-
telligible these declarations of GOD's Word, if
we regard them not as so many affirmations of
the great doctrine in question. Let not the reader turn away from GOD's Word. If he be a
disbeliever in the doctrine of Christ's vicarious
sufferings, let him be cautious how he tampers
with these solemn declarations. They affirm
the doctrine of the Atonement, or nothing at all.
They possess no meaning if interpreted in any
other light. Recur again to the amazing expressions :—"Wounded for our *transgressions.*"
"Bruised for our *iniquities.*" On Him the *iniquity* of us all." "Blood shed for the remission
of *sins.*" "Died for the *ungodly.*" "Made *sin.*"
"Through His blood the forgiveness of *sins.*"
"Propitiation for our *sins.*" What see we here,

but the Atoning blood—the full satisfaction—
the bearing of sin—the surety, the substitute ?

And how shall we account for the sufferings
of Christ, which were *intense*, and *mysterious*,
if not on the ground of their *vicarious* character?
Those sufferings were *intense* in the extreme.
There was a *severity* in them which, if not required by Divine Justice, would be perfectly un-
accountable. Heaven, Earth, and Hell, all were
in league against Him. Survey His eventful
history—mark every step which He took from
Bethlehem to Calvary; and what do we learn of
His sufferings, but that they were of the most
extraordinary and intense character. His ene-
mies, like dogs of war, were let loose upon Him.
His professed followers themselves, stood aghast
at the scenes through which their Lord was passing—one betraying Him, another denying Him,
and all, in the hour of His extremity, forsaking
Him. Is it any wonder that, in the anguish of
His soul, His suffering humanity should exclaim,
"Father, if it be possible, let this cup pass from
me, yet not my will, but thine be done." In that
awful moment, all the waves and billows of
God's wrath, due to the sins of His people, were

9

passing over Him. The Father, the last re-
source of sympathy, veiled His face, and with-
drew from Him His sensible presence, and on
the cross, draining the cup of sorrow, He fulfilled the prophecy which spake of Him—"I
have trodden the wine press alone ; and of the
people there was none with me." Isa. lxiii. 3.

His sufferings too, were *mysterious.* Why a
holy harmless Being,—whose whole life had
been one act of unparalleled benificence, should
be doomed to persecutions so severe, to sufferings so acute, and to a death so painful and ig-
nominious, the denier of the atonement must be
embarrassed to account. But the doctrine of a
vicarious sacrifice explains it all, and presents
the only key to the mystery. "He was made
sin for us who know no sin, that we might be
made the righteousness of GOD in Him." 2 Cor.
v. 21. "Christ hath redeemed us from the curse
of the law, being made a curse for us." Gal. iii.
13. All the mystery now is gone. He was
"made *sin* for us"—He was "made a *curse* for
us." He bore the sin, and consequently the
*penalty* of sin. Had we been left, Christian
*reader, to* bear our sins, we must inevitable have

borne alone the *punishment* of our sins.   But
Jesus took upon Him our sins.   For this, He
became a party in the covenant of redemption.
For this, He assumed our nature—For this, He
sorrowed in Gethsemane—For this, the law of
GOD exacted its utmost claim, and for this, the
justice of GOD inflicted the utmost penalty.   O
what a truth is this!  The Son of GOD offering
Himself up a sacrifice for sin!  He who knew
no sin; who was holy, harmless and undefiled;
not one thought of evil in His heart, yet made
sin, or a sin-offering!—O the bigness of the
thought!  If GOD had not Himself declared it,
we could have not believed it, though an angel's
trump had announced it.   GOD Himself must
proclaim it; and because He has so proclaimed
it, we believe it.   And GOD alone can write it
upon the heart.   'O thou blessed and adorable
Immanuel!  and was this the end and design of
thy intense and mysterious sufferings?   Was
it that thou shouldest obey, bear the sin, endure
the curse, and bow thy head in death, that I
might go free?   Was it in *my* stead, and in *my*
behalf?   O love unexampled!   O grace infinite
and free!   That GOD should become incarnate;

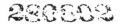

That the Holy One should so take upon Him
sin as to be dealt with by stern Justice, as though
He were Himself the sinner: That He should
drain the cup—give His back to the smiter—
endure the shame and the spitting, and at last
be suspended upon the cross, and pour out His
last drop of most precious blood, and all this for
*me*—for me a *rebel*—for me a *worm*—for me the
*chief of sinners !* Be astonished O heavens '! and
be amazed O earth! Was ever love like this ?'

It will now be appropriate to show from GOD's
Word, that the Atonement of the blessed Redeemer, was a *full* and *entire* blotting out of the
sins of the believer.   Need we say ought upon
the vast *importance* of this truth ? Need we say,
how closely it stands connected with the peace,
the sanctification, and the eternal glory, of the
sinner that hangs on Christ ? Let not the reader
be satisfied to rest upon the mere surface of the
truth, that Christ has made an atonement for sin.
This may be believed, and yet the full blessedness, peace and sanctification of it not enjoyed.
And why ? Because he enters not fully into the
*experience* of the truth.   Shall we not say too,
*because his* views of sin rest but on the surface

of sin's exceeding sinfulness? Deep views of sin,
will ever result in deep views of the Sacrifice
for sin. Inadequate knowledge of sin, inadequate knowledge of Christ. Low views of self,
high views of Christ. Be satisfied then not to
rest upon the surface of this wondrous truth.
May GOD the Eternal Spirit now lead us into it.

Before we consider the *completeness* of
Christ's atonement, it may be proper to glance
at the basis or cause of that completeness. This
arises from the infinite *dignity* of His Person.
His GODHEAD forms the basis of His perfect
work. It guarantees, so to speak, the glorious
result of His Atonement. It was this, that gave
perfection to His obedience, and virtue to His
Atonement. It was this that made the blood He
shed efficacious in the pardon of sin, and the
righteousness He wrought out complete in the
justification of the soul. His entire work would
have been wanting but for His GODHEAD. No
*created* Saviour—that dream of the Socinian—
could have given full satisfaction to an infinite
law, broken by man, and calling aloud for ven-
geance. How could such a sacrifice, as we
would *suppose* a created Saviour to offer, have

9*

"magnified the law, and made it honourable"!
utterly impossible! A finite being had broken it
—an infinite Being must repair it. An obedience was required, in every respect equal in
glory and dignity to the law that was violated.
The rights of the Divine government must be
maintained—the purity of the Divine nature
must be guarded—and the honour of the Divine
law must be vindicated. To accomplish this,
GOD Himself must become flesh, and to carry
this fully out, the incarnate GOD must *die!* O
depth of wisdom and of grace! O love infinite,
love rich, love free! Love

' Not to be thought on, but with tides of joy,
Not to be mentioned, but with shouts of praise.'

Stamped, as the work of Christ is, with the infinite glory and dignity of His GODHEAD, it will
now be an easy and a delightful task to trace
its perfection, as it is seen *first*, in the entire
blotting out of all sin, and *second*, in the complete justification of the person.

The PARDON of a believer's sins, is an *entire*
pardon. It is the full pardon of all his sins. It were
*no pardon* to him if it were not an entire pardon.

If it were but a partial blotting out of the thick cloud—if it were but a partial cancelling of the bond—if it were but a forgiveness of *some* sins only, then the gospel were no glad tidings to his soul. The law of GOD has brought Him in guilty of an entire violation. The justice of GOD demands a satisfaction equal to the enormity of the sins committed, and of the guilt incurred. The Holy Spirit has convinced him of his utter helplessness, his entire bankruptcy. What rapture would kindle in his bosom at the announcement of a *partial* atonement—of a *half* Saviour—of a *part* payment of the debt? Not one throb of joyous sensation would it produce. On the contrary, this very mockery of his wo, would but deepen the anguish of his spirit. But, go to the soul, weary and heavy laden with sin—mourning over its vileness, its helplessness, and proclaim the *Gospel.* Tell him that the Atonement which Jesus offered on Calvary, was a full satisfaction for his sins. That *all* his sins were borne and blotted out in that awful moment. That the bond which Divine Justice held against the sinner was *fully* cancelled by the obedience and sufferings of Christ, and that, appeased and

satisfied, GOD was "ready to pardon." How
beautiful will be the feet that convey to him
tidings transporting as this! And are not these
statements perfectly accordant with the declarations of GOD's own word? Let us ascertain.
What was the Ark symbollical of, alluded to by
the Apostle, in the ninth chapter of his Epistle
to the Hebrews, which contained the manna,
Aaron's rod, and the tables of the covenant, over
which stood the cherubims of glory shadowing
the mercy seat? What, but the entire covering
of sin? For, as the covering of the Ark did hide
the law and testimony, so did the Lord Jesus
Christ hide the sins of His chosen, covenant
people;—not from the eye of GOD's Omniscience,
but from the *eye of the law.* They stand legally
acquitted. So entire was the work of Jesus, so
infinite and satisfactory His obedience, the law
of GOD pronounces them acquitted—and can
never bring them into condemnation. "There
is therefore now no condemnation to them which
are in Christ Jesus; who walk not after the flesh,
but after the Spirit." Rom. viii. 1 "Who is he
that condemneth? It is Christ that died," &c.
How could the Apostle, with any truth, have

made a declaration so astounding, and uttered a challenge so dauntless as this, if the point, we are now endeavouring to establish, were not strictly as we affirm it to be?

And does not the *phraseology*, which the Holy Ghost employs in announcing the doctrine of Divine forgiveness, confirm the statement we have made? "I have blotted out, as a thick cloud, thy transgressions, and, as a cloud, thy sins: return unto me, for I have redeemed thee." Isa. xliv. 22. Where would be the constraining power of the motive to "return" to GOD, but on the ground of a full and entire blotting out of all sin? This it is, that subdues, overcomes, and wins back GOD's wandering child. This it is that abases the soul—deepens the conviction of its vileness, makes the sin of departure, of ingratitude, of rebellion, so abhorrent, when, on the broad basis of a full and free blotting out of sin, GOD bids the soul "return:"—' I have blotted all thy sins, *therefore* return. Though thou hast gone after other lovers—though thou hast departed from me—forgotten and forsaken me, yet have I blotted out, as a thick cloud, thy transgressions, return,

for I have redeemed thee.' Again, " In those
days, and in that time, saith the Lord, the iniquity of Israel shall be sought for, and there
shall be none ; and the sins of Judah, and they
shall not be found." Jer. l. 20. " He will turn
again, he will have compassion upon us ; he
will subdue our iniquities ; and thou wilt cast
ALL their sins into the depths of the sea." Mich.
vii. 19. What an astounding truth is contained
in these two passages ! In the one, it is declared,
that if the iniquity of Israel, and the sin of Judah,
be sought for, they shall not be found. So entire was the blotting out, so glorious was the
work of Jesus, so perfect His obedience, that if
the eye of GOD's holy law searches,—and where
can it not penetrate ?—it cannot discover them.
In the other, it is declared, that, so fathomless
are the depths of that sea of Atoning blood,
which Christ has poured out, that in it are cast,
never to be found again, ALL the sins of the believer. So that the trembling soul may exclaim,
" Thou hast, in love to my soul, delivered it
from the pit of corruption ; for thou hast cast
ALL my sins behind thy back." Isa. xxxviii. 17.

And who can read, without deep emotion, these

affecting announcements by the GOD of heaven? Gently chiding His wayward, yet beloved poople, He says, "But thou hast not called upon me, O Jacob; but thou hast been weary of me, O Israel. Thou hast not brought me the small cattle of thy burnt-offering, neither hast thou honoured me with thy sacrifices. I have not caused thee to serve with an offering, nor wearied thee with incense. Thou hast bought me no sweet cane with money, neither hast thou filled me with the fat of thy sacrifices; but thou hast made me to serve with thy sins, thou hast wearied me with thine iniquities. I, even I, am He that blotteth out thy transgressions for mine own sake, and will not remember thy sins." Isa. xliii. 22—25. "I will cleanse them from all their iniquity, whereby they have sinned against me, and I will pardon all their iniquities whereby they have sinned, and whereby they have transgressed against me." Jer. xxxiii. 8. "Bless the Lord, O my soul, and forget not all His benefits; Who forgiveth all thine iniquities; who healeth all thy diseases. For as the heaven is high above the earth, so great is his mercy toward them that fear Him. As far as the east is from

the west, so far hath he removed our transgressions from us." Psal. ciii 2, 3. 11, 12.   Look up,
ye saints of GOD, who are disconsolate through
fear of condemnation. See all your sins charged
to the account of your mighty Surety.   Yea,
see them all laid upon Him as your Substitute.
See Him bearing them away—sinking them in
the ocean of His blood—casting them behind
His back.   Look up and rejoice !  Let not the
indwelling of sin, the remains of corruption,
cause you to overlook this amazing truth,—*the
entire blotting out of all your sins, through the
atoning blood of your adorable Immanuel.*   It is
*truth,* and it is your privilege to live in the holy
enjoyment of it.   Fully received into the heart,
by the teaching of the Holy Spirit, its tendency
will be of the most holy, sanctifying, abasing
character.   It will weaken the power of sin—
it will draw up the heart in pantings for Divin
conformity—it will deaden the influence of tl
objects of sense—expel the love of the wo
and of self—impart tenderness to the conscien
and cause the soul to go softly,—" Walk
worthy of the Lord, unto all pleasing, b

fruitful in every good work, and increasing in the knowledge of God." Col. i. 10.

Before we pass to an experimental view of the kindred, though distinct doctrine of justification, we would beg the Christian reader's serious attention to a subject of the greatest importance, and yet one much overlooked,—we allude to the *intimate connection between a daily habit of confession of sin, and the application of the Atoning blood to the conscience.* This is a point of deep moment—and for the want of clear and scriptural views of it—or from not having seriously considered it at all, the believer in Christ walks for days, and it may be, months, without the blood upon the conscience. The sympathy between the soul's deep and humble confession of sin and the sense of the blotting out of that sin, is great. God has so ordained it. In turning to to the Book of Leviticus, xvi. 2, We find a beautiful and striking illustration of this important point. Thus we read:—"And Aaron shall lay both his hands upon the head of the live goat, and *confess* over him all the iniquities of the children of Israel, and all their transgressions in all their sins, putting them upon the head

*10*

of the goat, and shall *send them away* by the
hand of a fit man into the wilderness." Here
was the confession of sin and the pardon of sin,
closely and beautifully blended. The one would
have been useless if separated from the other.
There could be no pardon without confession,
and the mere confession, without the bearing
away of sin, would have availed nothing in
averting GOD's holy displeasure.

In the first Epistle of John, this Apostle thus
writes—Ver. 8, 9.—"If we say that we have no
sin, we deceive ourselves, and the truth is not
in us. If we *confess* our sins, He is faithful
and just to forgive us our sins, and to cleanse us
from all unrighteousness." Observe the close
relation in this passage ;—"If we *confess* our
sins, He is faithful and just to *forgive* us our
sins." Let us unfold some of the evils that result from a neglect of this duty, and some of the
blessings that result from its observance.

Sin unconfessed, *tends to remove that holy fa-
miliarity which ought always to subsist between*
GOD *and the believer.* This communion is of
the tenderest kind. The intercourse between a
*called,* pardoned, and adopted child, and its hea-

venly Father, is more close and endearing than
even that between a mother and her first born
child. Standing in the righteousness of the adorable Immanuel, the Father opens, without reser-
vation, all His heart—pours down the ocean
fulness of His love—communes by the inward
voice of the indwelling Spirit—and draws up the
affections to Himself. Who can fully enter into
that amazing expression of the Apostle's, "Beloved of GOD."? On GOD's part too, how precious is His own work in the soul of His child.
That lowly view of self,—that contrite sigh—that
broken heart—that faint and feeble longing for
Christ—that hungering and thirsting for righteousness—that poverty of spirit—those broken
accents of prayer—that feeble lisping of a child,
"Abba, Father !" O how unutterably dear is it all
to the heart of GOD ! But let the spiritual reader
imagine how much of this holy intercourse is
destroyed, and this confidence weakened, by the
remains of guilt upon the conscience, *through
the neglect of a full and free confession of sin.*
A sense of guilt upon the conscience invariably
occasions distant views of GOD. The moment
*Adam became* conscious of having sinned, he

hid himself from God's eye. He sought concealment from the endearing presence of Him, who had been wont to walk in the cool of evening through the bowers of paradise, in sweet and confiding communion. *It is so now.* Guilt upon the conscience, sin unconfessed, imparts misty, gloomy, distorted views of God. We lose that clear endearing view of His character, which we once had. We dare not look up with holy, humble, boldness. We misinterpret His dealings—think harshly of His ways—and if providences are dark, and afflictions come, in a moment we exclaim: 'I have sinned, and God is angry.' And so we seek concealment from God. We sink the father in the judge, and the child in the slave.

Another evil that results from sin unconfessed is, *the hardening tendency it produces upon the conscience.* To a child of God who has felt and mourned over the power of sin, we need not stay to prove, how hardening is the tendency of sin. —How it crusts the heart with a callousness which no human power can soften; and which often requires heavy affliction to remove. Where *a child of* God then, neglects the habit of a daily

confession of sin, by slow and almost impercep-
tible degrees, the conscience loses its tenderness, and becomes, by this gradual process, so
hardened, as at length to think nothing of a sin
which at one period would have filled the soul
with horror and remorse.

One more evil we may mention, and that is that,
a neglect of this most important duty, *causes a
fearful forgetfulness of sin, without the sweet sense
of its forgiveness.* The believer loses sight of his
sin, not because he knows it to be pardoned,
afresh blotted out, but from a mere carnal forgetfulness of the sin. The child of God on whose
conscience the atoning blood has been afresh
sprinkled, cannot soon forget his sin. O no!
Freed from a sense of its condemnation, delivered
from its guilt, and looking up to the unclouded
face of a reconciled God, he yet remembers how
far he could depart from the God that so loved
him, and so readily and freely forgave him.
The very pardon of his sin stamps it upon his
memory. He thinks of it, only to admire the
love, and adore the grace, and extol the blood
that blotted it out—and thus he is led to go softly
*all his days.* "My soul hath them still in re-
10*

membrance, and is humbled in me." Lam. iii.
20. But the believer who neglects the duty and
the privilege of confession, loses the remembrance of his sin, until brought under the rod of
the covenant ;—then some deep and heavy chastisement recalls it to his memory, and fills him
with shame, humiliation and confession. In this
state, the Eternal Spirit comes into the soul with
His *restoring* mercies, leads the abased and humbled believer afresh to the "fountain opened"—
GOD—the GOD of all comfort, speaks in language
of comfort and says, "I will establish my covenant with thee ; and thou shalt know that I am
the Lord : That thou mayest *remember*, and be
confounded, and never open thy mouth any more
because of thy shame, when I am pacified towards thee, for all that thou hast done, saith the
Lord GOD." Ezek. xvi. 62, 63.

The *blessings* that result from a strict *obser*
*vance* of daily confession of sin, are rich and v:
ried. We would present them as in one grou
  *The conscience retains its tender susceptibility*
*guilt.* Just as a breath will tarnish a mir
highly polished, so will the slightest abberrat
*of the heart* from GOD—the smallest sin, le:

its impression upon a conscience in the habit of a daily unburthening itself in confession, and of a daily washing in the fountain. Going thus to God, and acknowledging iniquity over the head of Immanuel—pleading the atoning blood—the conscience retains its tenderness—its sensativeness, and sin, all sin, is viewed as that which God hates, and the soul abhors.

This habit too, *keeps, so to speak, a clear account between* God *and the believer*. Sins daily and hourly committed are not forgotten—they fade not from the mind, and therefore they need not the correcting rod to recall them to remembrance. For let us not forget, God will eventually bring our sin to remembrance. "He will call to remembrance the iniquity." Ezek. xxi. 23. David had forgotten his sin against God, and his treacherous conduct to Uriah, until God sent the prophet Nathan to bring his iniquity to remembrance. A daily confession then of sin, a daily washing in the fountain, will preserve the believer from many and perhaps deep afflictions. This was David's testimony—"I *acknowledged* my sin unto thee, and mine iniquity have I not hid. *I said, I will confess my transgressions* unto the Lord, and thou *forgavest* the iniquity of my sin." Ps. xxxii. 5.

See then the close connexion between an honest and minute confession of sin, and the application of the precious blood of Christ. Let the child of GOD be encouraged to take all his sins to his heavenly Father. Have you sinned? Have you taken a single step in departure from GOD? Is there the slightest consciousness of guilt? go at once to the throne of grace—stay not till you find some secret place for confession—stay not till you are alone, lift up your heart *at once* to GOD, and confess your sin with the hand of faith upon the great atoning Sacrifice. Open all your heart to Him. Be not afraid of a full and honest confession. Shrink not from unfolding its most secret recesses—lay all bare before His eye. Do you think He will turn from the exposure? Do you think He will close His ear against your breathings. O no! Listen to His own encouraging, persuasive declarations—"Go and proclaim these words toward the north, and say, Return thou backsliding Israel, saith the Lord; and I will not cause mine anger to fall upon you: *for I am* merciful, saith the Lord, and I will not keep anger for ever. *Only acknowledge thine iniquity,* that thou hast transgressed against the Lord thy God." Jer. iii. 12, 13. "O Israel, return unto the Lord thy God, for thou hast fallen by thine iniquity. Take with you words, and turn to the Lord; say unto Him, Take away all iniquity, and receive us graciously." Hos. xiv. 1, 2.—"I will heal their backsliding, I will love them freely; for mine anger is turned away from him." Ver. 4. O what words are these! Does the eye of a poor *backslider* fall on this page? And as he now reads of GOD's readiness to pardon—of GOD's willingness to receive back the repenting prodigal, of His yearning after his wandering child, feels his heart melted—his soul subdued, and struck with that amazing declaration, "Only acknowledge thine iniquity," would dare creep down at His feet, and weep, and mourn, and confess. O is there one such now reading this page? then return, my brother, return! GOD,—the GOD against whom you have sinned, says, return. Thy *Father,*—the Father from whom you have wandered, is looking out for the first return of your soul, for the first kindlings *of godly* sorrow, for the first confes-

sion of sin. Return, my brother, return! GOD
has not turned His back upon you, though you
have turned your back upon Him. GOD has
not forgotten to be gracious, though you have
forgotten to be faithful. "I *remember* thee,"—
is His own touching language,—"the kindness of
thy youth, the love of thine espousals." Jer. ii.
2. O! then, come back, this moment, come
back; the fountain is still open—Jesus is still the
same—the blessed and Eternal Spirit, loving and
faithful as ever—GOD ready to pardon—take up
then the language of the prodigal and say, "I
will arise and go to my Father, and will say
unto Him, Father, I have sinned against heaven
and in thy sight, and am no more worthy to be
called thy son." "If we confess our sins, He is
faithful and just to forgive us our sins, and to
cleanse us from all unrighteousness."

We now proceed to show how full and entire
is the JUSTIFICATION of a believer. This will
not require much amplification—seeing that, if
the *pardon* of a believing sinner is a *full* and
*entire* forgiveness, it follows that, so must be
his *justification*. They both result from the
*same glorious* cause—the perfection of our
*adorable Lord's* obedience.

Let us briefly enquire what we are to understand by the *righteousness* of Christ, *imputed to
a believer*, and thus constituting the sole ground
of his acceptance. It is not our intention to
view the subject metaphysically, but in the clear
light of GOD's own Word. We deprecate the
introduction of a metaphysical and scholastic
mode of reasoning in the exhibition of Divine
truth. GOD's Word does not require it. It
is quite unnecessary in the investigation of
the mind of the Spirit. The *evils* too, resulting
from it, are many and dangerous. GOD's Word
is obscured, mystified, and often its simple
meaning fearfully perverted. The mind, in
search of the truth, not being able to follow a
metaphysical argument, or to comprehend the
meaning of a scholastic term, becomes perplexed,
embarrassed and discouraged, and at length
gives up the investigation. May it not be a
subject of important enquiry how far the pulpit
and the press, in their efforts to diffuse evangelical knowledge, may be chargeable with the
adoption of a mode of discussing religious truth,
far removed from the beautiful simplicity of the
Gospel, and *tending* to mar its beauty, pervert

its meaning, and impart to the learner crude and misty views of Divine truth? Confident are we, that that ministry would come clothed with most unction, and that treatise would be read with more blessing, and that believer would walk more in peace and joy in the Holy Ghost, where God's Word was most honoured, most prayerfully studied, and most studiously followed. This Book tells best and simplest, its own wondrous story. But to return from this digression.

We mean by justification, or rather, we would say, the Word of God means by Gospel justification, *the imputation of Christ's infinite and finished righteousness to a repenting, believing sinner.* The making over of His perfect obedience in behalf of His church, to him that believes. Christ obeyed not for Himself, but for His church. It is an absurdity to suppose that He obeyed the law for Himself. The law of God demanded no *personal* obedience from Christ; for He was perfectly holy—had never sinned, had never broken the law. And to suppose the law exacting obedience, and holding out its threats to a Being who was immaculately holy, and therefore had never incurred its penalty, is, to take a most obscure and defective view of truth.—True, Christ was made under the law, but it was "to redeem them that were under the law, that we might receive the adoption of sons." Gal. iv. 4, 5. If He was obligated to do ought for Himself, as under the personal curse of the law, then He became incarnate for *Himself*, obeyed for *Himself*, endured the curse for *Himself*, suffered for *Himself*, died and rose again for *Himself*.

As made under the law, true He was bound to obey, in its every iota, that law, but it was for the people for whom He had entered into a covenant engagement with the Father. In their behalf He kept the law—for it was not possible that He could Himself break it—Satan came, tried, and tempted Him, and found nothing in Him. John, xiv. 30. In their behalf He endured the curse, and suffered the penalty. And on the ground of His obedience,—His obedience, or righteousness imputed to them, in the same manner in which their sins were imputed to Him,—they stand before GOD, the holy, the heart-searching GOD, fully and freely "justified from all *things*." "For He hath made Him to be sin

11

for us, who knew no sin" (there is the *impu*
*tion* of our *sins* to Him) " that we might be m
the righteousness of God in Him"—(there is
*imputation* of His *righteousness* to us.) 2 Cor
21. " For such an high priest became us, w
is holy, harmless, undefiled, separate from sinn
and made higher than the heavens ; who ne
eth not daily as those high priests, to offer
sacrifice, first for his own sins, and then for
people's : for this He did once when He offe
up Himself." Heb. vii. 26, 27. With this
planation of the doctrine, let us proceed to
fold it.

The righteousness wrought out by the inc
nation, obedience, sufferings, and death of Chr
is a most glorious righteousness. It took in
' whole law of God. It did not soften down
ask for a compromise of its claims. It took
law in utmost strictness and honoured it.
gave all the law demanded, all it could dema
And what stamped this righteousness with
glory so great ? what enabled the Redeemer
offer an obedience so perfect ? what, but t
because He was God in our nature ! The L
*giver became* the Law fulfiller. The God beca

the Substitute—the Judge became the Surety.
Behold then, the justification of a believing sinner! He stands accepted in the righteousness of
Christ with *full* and *entire* acceptance.   What
says the Holy Ghost?  " In the Lord shall all
the seed of Israel be justified, and shall glory."
Is. xlv. 25. "And by Him, (the Lord Jesus,) all
that believe are justified FROM ALL THINGS, from
which ye could not be justified by the law of
Moses." Acts, xiii. 39. "Accepted in the Beloved." Eph. i. 6. " And ye are COMPLETE in
Him, which is the head of all principality and
power." Col. ii.10. " Christ loved the church,
and gave Himself for it, that He might sanctify
and cleanse it with the washing of water by the
Word, that He might present it to Himself a glorious church, not having spot or wrinkle, or any
such thing; but that it should be holy and without blemish."   Eph. v. 25—27.   "He hath made
Him to be sin for us, who knew no sin; that we
might be made the righteousness of God in
Him."   2 Cor. v. 21.   Mark the expression,
"MADE THE RIGHTEOUSNESS OF GOD!" So called,
because the righteousness which Christ wrought
out, was a *Divine* righteousness,—not the right-

eousness of a *created* being,—of an angel, or
a superior prophet, else it were blasphemy
call it "the righteousness of GOD."   O no!  1
righteousness in which you stand, if you  1
"accepted in the Beloved," is a more costly a
glorious righteousness than Adam's, or the hi;
est angel in glory,   It is "THE RIGHTEOUSNI
OF GOD.  The righteousness of the GODMAN,
possessing all the infinite merit, and glory, a
perfection of *Deity*.  And what seems still m(
incredible, the believer *is made the righteousn*
*of* GOD *in Christ*.  Made that righteousness,
that, beholding him in Christ, the Father (
"rest in His love, and rejoice over him w
singing." Zech. iii. 17.  Is it not then, we a
a *perfect*, a *complete* justification?  what can
more so?  Do not the passages, we have quot
prove it?  Can any other meaning be given
them, without divesting them of their beauty a
obvious sense?  Would it not be to turn fr
GOD's word, to dishonour and grieve the Spi
and to rob the believer of a most influential mot:
to holiness, were we to take a less expanc
view of this subject than that which we h;
*taken? Most* assuredly it would.  Then let (

Christian reader welcome this truth. If it is
God's truth,—and we humbly believe we have
proved it to be so,—it is not less his *privilege*
than his *duty* to receive it.

What consideration shall we urge upon him
wherefore he should welcome it? Shall we say,
his *sanctification* is intimately connected with it?
and what an argument should *this* be with a child
of God! To be holy—to be like God—to be con-
formed entirely to the will and image of Christ—
To have the temper, the taste; the principles, the
daily walk—all like our blessed Immanuel, who is
"the chief among ten thousands, the altogether
lovely." O! can a believer aspire to a more
lofty aim? And this righteousness,—this infinite,
this Divine, this finished righteousness, received
in the heart by God the Holy Ghost, broken up
to the soul, lived upon daily, will promote all this.
"In thy righteousness shall they be exalted."
Ps. lxxxix. 16. The righteousness of Christ
has a most *exalting* tendency. It exalts a believer's view of God, of His character and perfections. It exalts his view of Jesus, His person,
work, and love. It exalts the believer himself.
It *takes him out* of himself, above and beyond

*11**

himself.   It exalts his principles, his practice,
his affections, and conforms him to Christ.

· Shall we say his *happiness* is intimately connected with it? And where is the believer that
does not desire to walk *happily* with GOD?
This is the attainment, the world are eagerly in
search of; but the believer in Christ is its only
possessor.  He has found it, and found it in Jesus.
He has found it in a renunciation of self righteousness, and in a humble reception of Christ.
And there is no happiness, worthy of the name,
that is sought and found out of Jesus.   What
true happiness can the heart feel while it is unrenewed, its sins unpardoned, the soul unjustified,
and therefore under condemnation, and exposed
to the wrath of a holy and a just GOD? O dream
not of happiness, reader, until you have gone as
a repenting sinner to the cross of Christ.   Until
the atoning blood has been applied to your conscience, and the Spirit bears His witness to
your adoption.

If this, and this only, is the source of all true
happiness, then the more constantly and closely
the believer *realize* his full and complete acceptance in the Beloved, the greater must his hap-

piness be.  You may be a son or a daughter of
affliction.  In this furnace you may be chosen.
Is. xlviii. 10, and through this furnace—it may be
the Lord's holy will you should pass all your .
days.  You may be a child of poverty, possessing
but little of this poor world's comforts, lonely,
neglected, despised, yet, O look up !  You are
precious in GOD's sight,—dear to Him as the
apple of His eye—His heart yearns over you
with more than a Mother's exquisite fondness
for her child, because He has loved you with an
everlasting love, and to the praise of the glory
of His grace, has accepted you in the Beloved,
Eph. i. 6. *Realize* this, and though rough and
thorny may be your path, and fiery the furnace,
and deep your poverty, and lonely your situation,
you shall experience a peace, and a happiness,
to which the world around you is an utter
stranger,

Shall we say, the holy *influence* which a believer is called to exert around him, will be
greatly augmented, and powerfully felt, by an
abiding realization of His full and entire acceptance in Christ ?  The child of GOD is " the salt
of the earth"—" the light of the world."  He is

surrounded by moral putrefaction, and darkness. By his holy, consistent *example*, he is to exert a counteracting influence. He is to be purity where there is corruption, he is to be light where there is darkness. And if his walk is consistent, if his life is holy, his example tells, and tells powerfully, upon an ungodly world. Saints of God catch as it were, the contagion of his sanctity. The worldling acknowledges the reality of the gospel he professes, and the bold sceptic falls back abashed, and feels "how awful goodness is." What then will so elevate his own piety, and increase the power of His influence—as a realization of his justification by Christ? O how this *commends* the religion of Jesus! We will suppose a christian parent surrounded by a large circle of unconverted children. They look to him as to a living gospel. They look to him for an exemplification of the truth he believes. They expect to see its influence upon his principles, his temper, his affections, his whole conduct. What then must be their impression of the gospel if they behold their parent always indulging in doubts as to his acceptance, yielding to unbe-*lieving* fears as to his calling?—Instead of walking in the full assurance of faith, saying with the Apostle, "I *know* whom I have believed." 2 Tim. i. 12. Instead of walking in the holy liberty, peace and comfort of acceptance, there is naught but distrust, dread, and tormenting fear. How many a child has borne this testimony—"the doubts and fears of my parent, have been my great stumbling block." O then, for the sake of those around you—for the sake of your children, your connexions—your friends, your domesticks, *realise* your full, free and entire acceptance in Christ.

Is it any marvel then—reviewing our ground— that in speaking of His beloved and justified people, GOD employs in His Word language like this :—"Thou art all fair, my love ; there is no spot in thee." Cant. iv. 7. "He hath not beheld iniquity in Jacob, neither hath He seen perverseness in Israel." Numb. xxiii. 21. Carry out this thought. Had there been no *iniquity* in Jacob ? had there been no *perverseness* in Israel? Read their histories, and what do they develope but iniquity and perverseness of the most aggravated kind ? And yet that, GOD should say, He saw no *iniquity* in Jacob, and no perverseness in

Israel, what does it set forth, but the glorious work of the adorable Immanuel,—the glory, the fitness, the perfection of that righteousness, in which they stand "without spot, or wrinkle, or any such thing." Eph. v. 27. In themselves vile and worthless—sinful and perverse,—deeply conscious before GOD, of possessing not a claim upon His regard, but worthy only of His just displeasure, yet counted righteous in the righteousness of another,—fully and freely justified by Christ. Is this doctrine startling to some? Is it considered too great a truth to be received by others? Any other gospel than this, we solemnly affirm, will never save the soul! The obedience, sufferings, and death of the GODMAN, made over to the repenting believing sinner, by an act of free and sovereign grace, is the only plank on which the soul can safely rest. Let it attempt the passage across the cold river of death on any other, and it is gone! On this it may boldly venture, and on this it shall be safely and triumphantly carried into the quiet and peaceful haven of future and eternal blessedness. We acknowledge the *magnitude* of this doctrine. Yet *is it not to* be rejected because of its greatness.

It may be profound, almost too deeply so, for an angel's mind—The cherubim may veil their faces, overpowered with its glory, while yet, with eager longings, they desire to look into it—Still may the weakest saint of GOD receive it, live upon it, walk in it. It is "a deep river, through which an elephant might swim, and which a lamb might ford."

Nor let any individual slight it, because worldly men have *held it in unrighteousness*. To the heart of a child of GOD it should not be the less precious because of this. The abuse of any single truth is no argument against the soundness or utility of that truth. If so, then might we set aside well nigh every doctrine of the cross, because will nigh every doctrine of the cross has been abused to unholy purposes. It is a solemn thing for a believer to overlook any single doctrine, to stand aloof from any single truth of GOD's holy Word, because the pearl has been trampled under foot of swine—because ungodly men receiving the truth notionally in the judgment, and not experimentally in the heart, have walked after their own lusts, deceiving and deceived. *O no, we* look not to them for an exemplification of the great doctrines of grace; nor are we to attribute their abuse of God's truth to the legitimate tendency of the truth itself. This we assign as a reason why we contend so earnestly for *experimental religion*. There is no true holiness of heart, and of life, without it. The mere prater about doctrine, his head filled with notion, and his heart with pride and unmortified sin, may walk in the outward garb of Christianity, deceiving others,—and what at the day of judgment will be most awful—deceiving *himself;* but the day of *separation*, the day of *sifting*, will come, when the wheat will be gathered into the garner, and the chaff will be burnt with unquenchable fire.

Let not the reader then turn his back upon a truth, because unholy men have brought it into reproach—then might he turn his back upon Jesus, because of the wounds which, again and again, He has received in the house of His friends. The doctrine of God's eternal sovereign, and unconditional election of a people His redemption of them by the sacrifice of His Son, Jesus Christ, His particular and effect *calling* of them by the Eternal Spirit—the

complete pardon and justification, and their pre-
servation to eternal glory, these are GOD's truths
and not to be rejected.   They come *from* GOD,
and, when received in the heart, they lead *to*
GOD.   They have their origin in Him, and to
Him they draw the soul.   Precious truths!  How
they abase the sinner, how they exalt the dear
Redeemer.   How they glorify GOD, how they
empty, humble, and sanctify the soul.   We
would not be the individual to speak ought
against them, or think slightingly of them, no,
not for our right hand, or for our right eye.

And now, may we not enquire, have you, dear
reader, this robe upon you ?  In whose righteousness do you at this moment stand ?  Is it all profession merely ?  Startle not at the question—turn
not from it—it is for your life we ask it.   Do
you wonder that such a scrutiny into the ground
of your hope should be made ?  Are you astonished at the solemn fact implied in this question?
Be not so.   Many have lived the outward profession—have put on Christ in the external garb
—have talked well of Him—have been baptized in His name—given liberally for His cause,
and, *after all*, have gone into eternity, holding up

12

the empty lamp! O marvel not then, that we repeat the question,—*in whose righteousness do you at this moment stand?* Mere profession will not save your soul. Your being found mingling among the wise virgins will not secure you an admittance with them into heaven. Your talking respectfully of Jesus will avail you nothing. Your church memberships, your liberality, your irreproachable deportment, your spotless morality, your regular attendance on the sanctuary, all, all are vain without the justifying righteousness of the GODMAN upon you. What do you know of the broken heart, and the contrite spirit? What do you know of the healing blood of Jesus? What do you know of a sense of pardon and acceptance? What do you know of the witness of the Spirit? What do you know of a humble, low, abasing view of yourself? What do you know of a holy and a close walk with GOD? What do you know of communion and fellowship with the Fathe and His dear Son? In a word, what do y know of yourself as a helpless, ruined sinn and of Jesus as a rich, able, and present Savio Ponder these solemn questions. The hand *pens them,* trembles with awe as it traces t *on this* page. This is a day of great prof

—a day of great ingathering into the church. A day, when much chaff must necessarily be gathered with the wheat. It was so in the primitive days of the church, when Apostles, inspired by the Spirit of GOD, were the men who planted, watered, and gathered in the sheaves. Shall it then be thought a thing incredible with you that, in the *present day*, the minister may be deceived, and the hearer deceived, and neither of them know it? GOD is working wonders, we doubt not, in behalf of His American Israel—(may His *British* Israel share in the blessing!) yet it behoves us, the minister and the people—to move, with slow, cautious, and prayerful steps. It solemnly behoves each professing member of Christ's church, of every name and denomination, narrowly to scrutinize his motives—deeply to probe his heart—and closely and habitually to examine the foundation on which he is building for eternity. Thus shall he walk, if he be an adopted child, in the sweet and holy realization of his pardon and acceptance ;—thus shall he experience the blessedness of the man whose transgression is forgiven, whose sin is covered —and thus too, shall he constantly be "a vessel unto honour, sanctified, and meet for the master's use, and prepared unto every good work."

There are many and peculiar blessings which an experimental belief and realization of this great truth conveys into the soul, a slight glance at some of which, will close this chapter.

First, *A consciousness of perfect security, and freedom from condemnation.* Let us not be misunderstood. We mean not to affirm that, a child of GOD is secure *only* as he realizes his pardon and acceptance. Far be it from us to utter a sentiment like this. Many and long are the seasons of spiritual darkness, and sensible withdrawment's of GOD's presence, through which the believer is often called to pass. Seasons, during which his hope seems to have perished. Lam. iii. 18. And GOD, as he believes, has forgotten to be gracious. Ps. lxxvii. 9. Seasons, during which he cannot look up as a pardoned sinner, as a justified soul, as an adopted child, and say, "Abba Father!" All is midnight gloom to his soul. And while GOD seems to have withdrawn, satan instantly appears. Taking advantage of the momentary absence of the Lord,—for let it be remembered, it is not an *actual* and *eternal* withdrawment—he levels his fiery darts,—suggests hard thoughts of GOD—tempts the soul to believe the past has been but a deception, and that the future will develope nothing but darkness and despair.  Satan, that constant and subtle foe, frequently seizes too, upon periods of the believer's history, when the providences of GOD are dark and mysterious—when the path, along which the weary pilgrim is pressing, is rough and intricate —or, it may be, when he sees not a spot before him—the way is obstructed, and he is ready to exclaim with Job, "He hath fenced up my way that I cannot pass, and He hath set darkness in my paths"—Job, xix. 8. Or with Jeremiah, "He hath hedged me about, that I cannot get out." Lam. iii. 7. Let it not then be forgotten by the soul that walks in darkness and has no light, that the providential dealings of a covenant GOD and Father, which now are depressing the spirits, stirring up unbelief, and casting a shade over every prospect, may be seized upon by its great enemy, and appropriated to an occasion of deep and sore temptation.  It was thus he dealt with our blessed Lord, who was in all points tempted as His people, yet without sin. Heb. iv. 15.

12*

Satan, taking advantage of his prolonged fast, and the weakness of body and hunger which were the consequence—for let it ever be borne in mind, GOD took upon Him *pure humanity* with all the sympathies of our nature,—and with all the weaknesses which clung to it—presented the temptation in its most pliable form. Luke, iv. 2—13. And if the Head thus was tempted, so will be the member—if the Lord, so the disciple. And for this very end was our blessed Lord thus tempted, that He might enter sympathetically into all the circumstances of His tried and suffering people—"For in that He Himself hath suffered being tempted, He is able to succour them that are tempted." Heb. ii. 18.

But we must not, we dare not, refrain from ascribing this spiritual darkness to another, and perhaps more obvious cause,—we allude to *a distant and careless walk.* This will as certainly bring darkness into the the soul, with its painful attendants—unbelief—loss of evidence—hard thoughts of GOD—slavish fear—as if an individual were to close every inlet of a habitation to the rays of the sun, and sit down amidst the *gloom* and the obscurity with which he has enshrouded himself. There is no true spiritual light but that which beams from the Sun of Righteousness; and to this every inlet of the soul must be open. All other light is false—it is but like the treacherous beacon erected upon a rock-bound coast, for the purpose of beguiling to its shore the unsuspecting barque. To enjoy this light then, a believer must dwell near the Sun—he must live close to Christ. He must live the life of daily faith upon Him,—He must look away from Himself to Jesus,—He must walk worthy of the Lord unto all pleasing,—he must be found prayerful and diligent in the means, while rising above them, he draws all his light, life and peace from the GOD of the means. O what losers are they who walk as Peter walked,—*at a distance* from their Lord—what seasons of endearing communion—what tokens of love—what visits of mercy they rob themselves of. What lovers are they who neglect the means of grace—closet prayer—church fellowship—the communion of saints—the blessed ordinances of baptism and the Lord's supper,—these channels through which a covenant GOD conveys such untold blessings into the soul of His dear child—for "the secret of the Lord is with them that fear Him;" and to *fear* Him, is not to dread Him as a slave, but as a child to walk in all the commandments and ordinances of the Lord blameless,—O! what losers then are such!

While penning this closing part of the chapter, the writer was sent for to administer spiritual consolation to one on the confines of eternity, who, at, an early period of her life, professed publicly her attachment to the Lord, but who, after a time, walked no more with Jesus—and now the season of sickness, and probably of death, had come! And O! could he have gathered every wandering, every backsliding, every careless, worldly professor of Christ around that bed, to have listened to the deep regrets, the bitter self reproaches, the piercing cries for pardon that fell from her lips, and to have witnessed too, the deep anguish that wrung her agonized bosom, how more powerfully would they have warned, and how more persuasively would they have plead, than the page which now warns and pleads with the careless, prayerless, worldly professor. Christian professor! are you walking at a distance from Christ, if following Him at all? Are you open-

ing your heart to the world—laying yourself out
for its entanglements? Are you conforming to it
in your spirit, your policy, your maxims, your
dress, your pursuits, your friendship, your religion? Are you neglecting the means of grace,
the sanctuary of GOD—the preaching of the
gospel, the social prayer meetings, the communion of saints? Are you neglecting prayer—
family prayer—social prayer—sanctuary prayer,
—most of all, *closet* prayer? O, if so, how fearfully you are turning your back upon GOD. How
wantonly are you trampling your precious privileges under foot. What a harvest of sorrow
are you sowing for a dying hour. What reason
have you to tremble, least after all, Christ has
never been formed in your heart the hope of
glory, What is your *present* hope? Is it only
a profession? Give it up—abandon it as worthless, and as a sinner undone, a sinner without a
hope, go to Jesus. A mere profession will never
save you. A bear supposition will only de-
lude you. You must have *the witness of the
Spirit.* But to the soul following hard after
GOD, we would say, there are two 'exceeding
great and precious promises,' which a child of
*God should ever* keep in view ;—"Unto the up-

right there ariseth light in the darkness." Ps.
cxii. 4. "Unto you that fear my name, shall
the Sun of Righteousness arise with healing in
His wings." Mal. iv. 2. Thus is it evident
that, to those who walk *uprightly* before GOD;—
upright in heart, as well as upright in outward
conduct; upright in principle as well as upright
in practice, and to those who walk in the holy
filial fear of GOD, the Lord has His choicest
covenant blessings. But to return.

We say not then, that a momentary sense of
GOD's withdrawment from the believer, affects
his actual security in the atoning blood. This,
nothing can disturb. The safety of a child of
GOD hinges not upon a frame or a feeling, the
ever varying and fitful pulses of a believing soul
—O no! The covenant rest upon a surer basis
than this. The child of the covenant is sealed
with a better hope and promise. *He* may change,
but his covenant GOD never. *His* feelings may
vary, but His Father's love never veers. He
loved him *from* all eternity, and that love extends
*to* all eternity. As GOD never loved His child
for ought He saw, or should see, in that child, so
His love never changes for all the fickleness, sin-

fulness and unworthiness He daily and hourly discovers. O where would the soul fly but for this truth! When it takes into account the sins, the follies, the departures, the flaws of but one week—yea, when it reviews the history of but one day, and sees enough sin in a thought to sink it to eternal and just perdition, but for an unchangeable GOD, to what consolation would it resort?

But what forms the great security of the believer? what, but the *atoning blood*? This, and this only. The Father, beholding His child in His beloved Son, washed and clothed—pardoned and justified, can "rest in His love, and joy over him with singing." The Atonement guarantees his eternal safety. What formed the security of Noah and his family, when the deluge of GOD's wrath descended upon an ungodly world? The *Ark* in which GOD had shut him. What formed the security of the children of Israel in Egypt, when the destroying angel passed through the camp waving in his hand the weapon of death? The *blood of the pascal lamb*, sprinkled on the lintel and door posts of their dwellings; and where this sacred sign was seen, into that house he dared not enter, but passed on to do the work of death where no blood was found. Exactly what the Ark was to Noah, and the blood of the lamb was to the children of Israel, is the atoning blood of Christ to the believing soul. *It forms his eternal security.* Reader! is that blood applied to you? Are you washed in it? Is it upon you at this moment? Precious blood! Precious Saviour who shed it! Precious faith that leads to it! How it washes away all sin;—how it lightens the conscience of its burthen,—heals the heart of its wound,—dispels the mist, and brings down the full unclouded sunlight of GOD's reconciled countenance in the soul. O! adore the love, and admire the grace that opened the fountain, and led you to bathe, all guilty, polluted, and helpless as you were, beneath its cleansing stream.—And with Cowper let us sing,

> "E're since by faith I saw the stream
> Thy flowing wounds supply,
> Redeeming love has been my theme,
> And shall be till I die."

> "Then in a nobler, sweeter song,
> I'll sing thy power to save;
> When this poor lisping, stammering tongue
> *Lies* silent in the grave."

Second, *deeper views of sin's exceeding sinfulness*, may be regarded as another invaluable blessing, resulting from a realizing apprehension of the atoning blood.  No child of GOD, if he is advancing in the Divine life, but must mourn over his defective views of sin.  The holier he grows, the more sensible is he of this.  Yea, may we not add, the deeper the view of his own vileness, the stronger the evidence of his growth in sanctification.  A growing hatred of sin, of *little* sins, of *great* sins, of *all* sin;—sin detected in the indwelling principle, as well as sin observable in the outward practice,—O, it is one of the surest symptoms of the onward progress of the soul in its spiritual course.  The believer himself may not be sensible of it, but others see it.  To him it may be like a retrograde, to an observer it is an evidence of *advance*.  The child of GOD is not the best judge of his own spiritual growth.  He may be rapidly advancing when not sensible of it.  The tree may be growing downwards—its roots may be expanding and grasping more firmly the soil in which they are concealed, and yet the appearance of growth be not very apparent.  There is an inward, con-

13

cealed, yet *effectual* growth of grace in the soul
—The believer may not be sensible of it, and
even others may overlook it—but GOD sees it.
It is His own work, and He does not think meanly
of it. GOD, in His gracious dealings with the believer, often works, by *contraries*. He opens the eye
of His child to the deep depravity of the heart—
discloses to him the chamber of imagery—re-
veals to him the sin, unthought of, unsuspected,
unrepented, unconfessed, that lies deeply em-
bedded there—and why? only to make His
child more holy.  To compel him to repair to
the mercy seat, there to cry, there to plead, there
to wrestle for its subjection, its mortification, its
crucifixion.  And through this, as it were, cir-
cuitous process, the believer presses on to high
and higher degrees of holiness.  In this way too,
the believer earnestly seeks for *humility*, by a
deep discovery which the Lord gives him of the
*pride* of his heart,—for *meekness* by a discovery
of *petulance* ;—of *resignation* to GOD's will, by a
sense of *restlessness* and *impatience*, and so on,
through all the graces of the blessed Spirit.
Thus there be a great growth in grace, when a
*believer's* views of sin's exceeding sinfulness,
and the inward plague, are deepening.

But how are these views of sin to be deepened? By constant, close views of the blood of Christ;—realizing apprehensions of the atonement. This is the only glass through which sin is seen in its greatest magnitude. Let the Christian reader then, deal much and often with the blood of Christ. O! that we should need to be urged to this. That once having bathed in the "fountain opened," we should ever look to any other mode of healing, and of sanctification. For let it never be forgotten that, a child of God is as much called to live on Christ for *sanctification* as for *pardon.* "Sanctify them through thy truth." And who is the truth? Jesus Himself answers, "I am the truth." Then we are to live on Jesus for *sanctification.* And happy and holy is he who thus lives on Jesus. The fulness of grace that is treasured up in Christ, why is it there? For the *sanctification* of His people. For the *subduing* of all their sins. O forget not then that, He is the *Refiner* as well as the *Saviour.* The *Sanctifier* as well as the *Redeemer.* Take your indwelling corruptions to Him—Take the easy besetting sin—the weakness, the infirmity, of whatever nature it is, at once to Jesus, His grace can make you all that He would have you to be. Remember too, that this is one of the great privileges of the life of faith,—*living on Christ for the daily subduing of all sin.* This is the faith that purifies the heart, and it purifies by leading the believer to live out of himself upon Christ. To this blessed and holy life our Lord Jesus referred, when speaking of its necessity in order to the spiritual fruitfulness of the believer—"Abide in me, and I in you. As the branch cannot bear fruit of itself except it abide in the vine; no more can ye except ye abide in me. I am the the vine ye are the branches; he that abideth in me, and I in him, the same bringeth forth much fruit; for without me ye can do nothing." John, xv. 4, 5.

O that the church of Christ, and each individual member, would but realize this truth, that simpler, closer, more experimental views of Jesus would essentially strengthen the tone of inward spirituality and comfort. The great secret of all comfort in seasons of affliction, is to take the affliction as it comes, simply to Christ; and the great secret of all holiness is to take *the corruption* as it rises, simply to Christ. It is this *living upon Christ for all he needs*, this going to Christ under all circumstances, and at all seasons, which forms the happy and holy life of a child of GOD: There is no other path for him to walk in. The moment he turns from Christ, he becomes like a vessel loosed from its moorings, and driven at the mercy of the winds from billow to billow. Christ must be all in all to him. Friends, domestic comforts, church privileges, ordinances, means of grace, nothing must suffice for Jesus. And why does the Lord so frequently discipline the soul?—why remove friends, why blight domestic comforts, why rob us of church privileges, why close up the ordinances, and write death upon the means of grace, O why, but to open a way through which He Himself might enter the believer, and convince that lonely, bereaved, and desolate heart, that He is a substitute for every thing, while nothing shall ever be a substitute for Him. He will have the *supreme* affection of His saints,—they shall find their all in Him, and to this end He sends afflictions, crosses and disappointments ments, but to wean them from their idols, and draw them to Himself.

13*

Sometimes, in order to learn experimentally this holy truth, that Christ must be every thing, the Lord, the Spirit, leads back the believer to *first principles.* He is led to retrace his steps, go over the ground he has travelled, and find his comfort and his evidence at the very spot from whence he first set out. He has to come, *as at first,* a poor, empty, helpless sinner, hanging on a full, rich, and all-sufficient Saviour. After all he has passed through of severe trial and fiery temptation, after all the storms and tempests, the conflicts and the victories, he is compelled to betake himself afresh to Jesus, empty and helpless as when first he cried for mercy. This, let us assure the reader, is no small proof of GOD's love, thus to be led back to first principles. Let him not be discouraged if the Lord is dealing thus with him now. Let him count it all joy if his Great Teacher has seen fit to put him in a lower class, and has given him the first lesson of Christian experience to learn—That lesson is the first and the last lesson. Happy and holy is he who thoroughly learns it.*

* The Author will not soon lose the impression left upon his mind *by an interview with* that eminent servant of Christ, the late Rev.

Third,—*A conformity to the death of Christ,* may be regarded as another, and a great blessing, resulting from a personal realization of the atoning blood. Indeed, we dare affirm that, conformity to His death, can only be obtained by close, individual, realizing views of the cross. It is in the cross sin is seen in its exceeding sinfulness. It is in the cross the holiness of GOD shines with such ineffable lustre. This is the sun that throws its light upon these two great objects—the holiness of GOD—the sinfulness of the sinner. Veil this sun—remove the cross, blot out the Atonement and all our knowledge of holiness and sin vanishes into distant and shadowy views. Faith, dealing much and closely with the cross of Christ, will invariably produce in the soul, conformity to His death. This was the great desire of the apostle. "That I may know Him, and the power of His resurrection, and the fellowship of His

---

Rowland Hill, a few months previous to his death, who, when speaking of his then state of mind, remarked in his peculiarly solemn manner,—" Sir, when I enter heaven, I shall enter it, crying 'God be merciful to me a sinner.' " Coming from such a man, and at such a time, it was an affecting and striking testimony to the blessedness *of being led back to first principles.*

sufferings, being made conformable to His death."
Philipp. iii. 10. This was the noble prayer of
this holy man. He desired crucifixion with
Christ. A crucifixion to sin, to indwelling sin—
to sin in its every shape—to sin in principle,
sin in temper, sin in worldly conformity, sin in
conversation, sin in thought, yea, sin in the very
glance of the eye. He desired not only a crucifixion of sin, of one particular sin, but of *all*.
sin—not only the sin that most easily beset him,
the sin that he daily saw and felt, and mourned
over, but the sin that no eye saw but GOD's—
the sin of the *indwelling principle*,—the root of
all sin—*the sin of his nature*. This is to have
fellowship with Christ in His sufferings. Jesus
suffered as much for the *subduing* of the indwelling principle of sin, as for the *pardon* of
the outbreakings of that sin in the daily practice.
Have we fellowship with Him in these sufferings? *There must be a crucifixion of the indwelling power of sin.*—To illustrate the idea,
—if the *root* be allowed to strengthen, and expand, and take a deeper and firmer grasp, what
more can we expect, than that the *tree* will
*shoot* upward, and branch out on either hand.

To cut off the outward branches is not the proper method to stay the growth of the tree. The root must be uncovered, and the axe laid to it. *Outward* sins may be cut off, and even honestly confessed and mourned over, while the *concealed principle*, the *root* of the sin is overlooked, neglected, and suffered to gather strength and expansion.

That the inherent evil of a believer will ever, in his present existence, be entirely eradicated, we do not assert. To expect this, would be to expect what God's word has not declared. But that it may be greatly *subdued* and *conquered,*— its power *weakened* and *mortified,* this, the word of God leads us to hope for, and aim after. How is this to be attained? Faith dealing frequently and closely with Christ—The Atoning blood upon the conscience—The "fountain opened" daily resorted to—The believer sitting constantly at the foot of the cross—gazing upon it with an eye of steady, unwavering faith,— "looking unto Jesus." In this posture, sin, *all* sin—the sin of the heart, the sin of the practice is mourned over, wept over, confessed, mortified, crucified. Let the reader again be re-

minded that, all true crucifixion of sin springs
from the cross of Christ.

Fourth,—*A most powerful incentive to prayer*,
is found in a close and realizing view of the
atoning blood. What encouragement does it
present to this blessed and holy life of communion with GOD! The atoning blood! The mercy
seat sprinkled over! The High Priest before the
throne! The cloud of incense constantly ascending! The Father well pleased! What can
more freely invite the soul that pants for close
and holy intercourse with GOD? And when the
atoning blood is realized upon the conscience,
—when pardon and acceptance are sealed upon
the heart by the Eternal Spirit, O then, what a
persuasion to draw nigh the throne of grace has
the believer in Christ. Then, there is no consciousness of guilt to keep the believer back.
No dread of GOD. No trembling apprehensions
of a repulse. GOD is viewed through the cross,
as *reconciled*, and as standing in the endeared
relationship, and wearing the inviting smile, of
a *Father*. With such an altar, such a High
Priest, such atoning blood, and such a reconciled GOD, what an element should *prayer* be to

a believer in Christ! Let the soul, depressed, burthened, tried, tempted as it may be, draw nigh the mercy seat. GOD delights to hear, delights to answer. Taking in the hand the atoning blood—pleading the infinite merit of Christ —reminding the Father of what His Son has accomplished—of His own gracious promise to receive and favourably answer the petition endorsed with the name, and presented in behalf of that Son, the feeblest child of GOD—the most disconsolate, the most burthened, may approach, and open all the heart to a prayer hearing and prayer answering GOD. Let the atoning blood be strenuously pleaded. Let the precious and infinite merit of Christ be fully urged, and the blessing petitioned for will be obtained.

May not this be assigned as a reason why so few of our petitions are answered—why so little blessing is obtained—*the faint pleading of the atoning blood?* There is so feeble a recognition of the blessed way of access. So little wrestling with the precious blood. So little looking by faith to the cross. The dear name of Immanuel so seldom urged, and when urged, so coldly mentioned,—O is it any marvel that our prayers return to us unanswered—the petition ungranted —the draft on the full treasury of His love unhonored. The Father loves to be reminded of His beloved Son. The very breathing of the name, to Him is music. The very waving of the censor of infinite merits to Him is fragrant. He delights to be pressed with this plea. It is a plea at all times prevalent. It is a plea He cannot reject. It glorifies Himself, honours His Son, while it enriches him who urges it. And O, in the absence of all other pleas, what a mercy to come with a plea like this! Who can fully estimate it? No plea has the poor believer, springing from himself. He searches, but nothing can he find on which to rest a claim. All within is vile, all without is marred by sin. Unfaithfulness, ingratitude, departure, do but make up the history of the day. But *in Christ*, he sees that which he can urge, and in urging which, GOD will hear and answer. "Having therefore, brethren, boldness to enter into the holiest by the blood of Jesus, by a new and living way which He hath consecrated for us, through the veil, that is to say, His flesh; And having an *High* priest over the house of GOD; let us draw near with a true heart in full assurance of faith, having our hearts sprinkled from an evil conscience, and our bodies washed with pure water." Heb. x. 19—22.

Fifth,—We would allude but to one other blessing growing out of the Atonement realized —*the spring it gives to all holy evangelical obedience*. The great impelling motive of all gospel obedience is, *the love of Christ in the heart*. David acknowledged this principle when he prayed, "I will run the way of thy commandments, when thou shalt enlarge my heart." Ps. cxix. 32. The Apostle admits it when he says, "the love of Christ constraineth us." In order to walk as an obedient child—to bear the daily cross—to honour the institution, and yield obedience to the law of Christ—to delight in the precepts as in the doctrines of God's truth, *the atoning blood must be realized*. How easy and how sweet will then become the commandments of the Lord. Duties will be viewed as privileges —and the yoke felt to be no yoke, and the cross to be no cross.

If these are the inestimable blessings connected with *personal*, and close realizing views

14

of the blood of atonement, surely the Christian reader will strive to live near the fountain. This is the only spot where his soul shall flourish. As the gentle flower which blooms unseen by the side of some veiled fountain, is, from the constant moisture it receives always beautiful and fragrant, so is that believing soul the most fruitful, holy, spiritual and devoted, who daily dwells by the side, yea, *in* the "fountain opened for sin and uncleanness." We see not how a child of God can be fruitful otherwise. A sweet and abiding consciousness of pardon and acceptance, is essential to spiritual fruitfulness. No believer can advance in the Divine life—wage a daily war with the innumerable foes that appose him—and be fruitful in every good work, who is perpetually in search of evidence of his adoption. We need all our time, all our energies, all our means in order to vanquish the spiritual philistines who obstruct our way to the heavenly Canaan. We have none to send in search of evidences, least while they have gone the bridegroom cometh! O *then* to know that all is right. The thick cloud blotted out—the soul *wrapped in* the robe of righteousness—*ready to*

enter into the marriage supper of the Lamb.
To die, will be quite enough.  To face, and
grapple with the king of terrors will be sufficient
employment for the spirit struggling to be free.
No time, no strength, no energy then to search
for evidences.  Let not the professor of Christ
leave the "sealing" of his pardon and acceptance
to that fearful hour; but let him earnestly seek
*it now*, that when he comes to die, he may have
nothing to do, *but to die*.  And that will be quite
enough.

# CHAPTER IV.

## THE FREENESS OF THE ATONEMENT.

### THE ANXIOUS SINNER VENTURING ON CHRIST.

*" Being justified freely by His grace, through the redemption that is in Christ Jesus." Rom. iii. 24.*

WHEN speaking of the great unfolding of Divine mercy in the redemption by Christ, the Apostle employs language the most concise and expressive;—he terms it, "The grace of God that bringeth salvation." Tit. ii. 2. In this short but emphatic sentence, he elevates his reader at once to the source and fountain head of all grace. He sets forth its author—its nature—and its end. It is the GRACE *of* GOD,—constituting as essential and substantial a part of the Divine existence, as the attributes of power, holiness, justice or goodness. With an eminent divine, we would pass to higher ground even than this. We would rather not call it an attribute, but the WILL of GOD which brings all other manifesta*tions of* the Divine character before the eye.

"It is not mercy; though mercy is to be seen in grace; it is not holiness, though holiness is to be seen in grace; it is a mere act of the Divine will, which manifests itself to all it pleases. It is necessary to go still higher: it is not merely the second in a series of ascending steps; it is not a repairing of a breach; but an exalting of the handyworks of God into a higher region; in humanity to make the GODHEAD forever manifest and to lift man up, and make him the nearest link in that chain that hangs from the throne of GOD."

A less theological, and perhaps more simple definition of grace may be acceptable to the general reader. And as the great MANIFESTATION of this grace we are now to consider, is *the Atonement of Christ,* we prefer the phrase the *'freeness* of the Atonement,' as expressing, " the grace of GOD that bringeth salvation." Should not even this be deemed sufficiently explicit, we mean then, *the perfectly gratuitous and unconditional manner, in which the blessing of pardon and justification, flowing through the atonement of Christ, come to the vilest sinner, sensible of his lost state, and made willing to accept of Jesus*

14*

*in the day of God's mighty power.* We enter
the more readily on the discussion of this subject, not only from a deep consciousness of its
vast importance, but also from the conviction,
which much conversation with inquiring souls
has tended to deepen, that, from the want of
clear and spiritual views of the *freeness* of the
gift, the perfectly *unconditional* bestowment of
the blessing, many are kept, even among those
"called to be saints," from entering fully into
the liberty and peace of the gospel. They have
been convinced of their need of Christ—They
have been made to hunger and thirst for pardon
and acceptance—They have been brought, it
may be, through a deep 'law work of the soul,'
to stand, as on the very borders of the land that
flows with milk and honey, but looking more to
themselves and less to Christ,—lingering on its
margin, while the river flows so richly and so
freely at their feet, waiting for some *condition*
to be performed, some *fitness* to be experienced,
or some some *price* to bring, they are kept back
from those rich and untold blessings which a
closing in with Jesus the Saviour of sinners
*would* assuredly bring into their possession.

For the purpose of clearness in the discussion of our subject, the reader will be first led to consider the simple and express testimony of GOD's Word—then, the *medium* through which its blessings flow to the seeking soul :—and lastly, some scriptural *examples* will be adduced confirmatory of the doctrine before us. In the observation now to be made, we particularly address ourselves to that class of our readers who, with brokenness of heart and deep contrition of spirit are inquiring, "what shall I do to be saved ?" With you dear penitent reader, the anxious question is, "will GOD have mercy upon *me*. Will He save a wrech so vile as *I* ?" Read then, with close attention and prayer, the following statement, and may the Eternal Spirit give you light, joy and peace !

In adducing the simple and express testimony of GOD's word on this subject, let not the reader be amazed if we lead him first into the *Old Testament.* For where will be found more distinct and glorious views of the atonement—its nature, design and freeness, than are found in the Old Testament writings ? The single point of course now under *proof* is, the perfect freeness of the gift. This is the testimony. "Ho, every one that thirsteth, come ye to the waters, and he that hath no money; come ye, buy and eat; yea, come, buy wine and milk without money, and without price." Isa. lv. 1. Behold the *freeness* of the rich and inestimable blessing! "Without money—without price." The simple meaning of which is—without *worthiness*, without *fitness* —without *condition.* So that the most unworthy, the most vile, the most penniless may come and drink water freely out of the wells of salvation. This is the language of GOD by the mouth of His prophets; what a gospel then is here revealed! How full the supply! how free the gift! And if this was the language of GOD under the obscure exhibition of the gospel, what must be His free welcome to poor sinners under the full, meridian glory of the gospel? Now that Christ has come, and the atonement has been made, and the fountain has been opened, and the invitation has gone out, can we suppose that the blessing of pardon will be less freely bestowed?

Again,—"Thus saith the Lord, ye have sold yourselves for nought, and ye shall be redeemed *without money.*" Isa. lii. 3. Again, "The Spirit of the Lord God is upon me ; because the Lord hath anointed me to preach good tidings unto the meek : He hath sent me to bind up the broken-hearted, to proclaim liberty to the captives, and the opening of the prison to them that are bound." Isa. lvi. 1. Mark the expressions as descriptive of the characters to whom our blessed Lord came, "broken-hearted"—"captives,"—"them that are bound." Where was there worthiness here? What price with which to purchase their redemption, had these 'broken-hearted,' these 'captives,' these 'bound?' See then reader, how the glorious atonement received its stamp of *freeness*, even under the legal dispensation. Come we now to the clearer revelations of the new Dispensation.

Take those remarkable words—"and when they had nothing to pay, he frankly forgave them both." Luke, vii. 42. O sweet expression ! '*Nothing to pay.*' Entirely bankrupt. Poor, wretched, penniless, bereft of all—nothing to pay, and yet *frankly forgiven;* i.e. fully, freely, cordially forgiven ;—*forgiven with all the heart of God.* But one other passage is adduced. "And the Spirit and the bride say come. And

let him that heareth say come. And let him
that is athirst, come: and whosoever will, let
him take the water of life *freely*." Rev. xxii.
17. See how the Word of GOD closes with the
proclamation of a free grace salvation. The
last words that linger in sweet vibration on the
ear, as the blessed canon of scripture closes are,
"*the water of life freely* !" Let us view the subject in another point of light.

If it be shown from GOD's truth, that *faith*, and
not the works of the law, is the grand medium
through which pardon and justification flow,
then, even as faith is the gift of GOD's grace, it
will be clear that, in this respect, the atonement
must be *free* and *unconditional.* What saith
the scripture ? " Therefore by the deeds of the
law there shall no flesh be justified in His sight:
for by the law is the knowledge of sin. But
now the righteousness of GOD without the law
is manifested, being witnessed by the law and
the prophets ; even the righteousness of GOD
which is by *faith* of Jesus Christ unto all and
upon all them that *believe :* for there is no difference. For all have sinned and come short of
*the glory* of GOD ; Being freely justified by His

grace through the redemption that is in Christ Jesus: Whom GOD hath set forth to be a propitiation *through faith* in His blood, to declare His righteousness for the remission of sins that are past, through the forbearance of GOD! To declare, I say, at this time His righteousness: that he might be just, and the justifier of him which *believeth* in Jesus. Where is boasting then? It is excluded. By what law? Of works? Nay: but by the law of *faith*. Therefore we conclude that a man is justified by *faith* without the deeds of the law." Rom. iii. 20—28. Thus, by one of the finest arguments in the apostolic writings, does Paul triumphantly establish the perfect freeness and unconditional character of a sinner's acceptance with God. Review the outline of his reasoning. "By the deeds of the law there shall no flesh be justified." By "the deeds of the law," he has reference to those many and fruitless efforts to obey the law which men in a state of nature are found so zealously to aim at. Are you striving, reader, to conform to the requirement of this holy, this inflexible law of GOD? Let me assure you, that all these strivings, all those works, all that toiling is worse than worth-

less in God's holy sight—they are *sinful,*—they
proceed from an *unregenerate* nature, from an
*unrenewed, unsanctified* heart—They flow not
from faith and love; and therefore the heart
being thus a fountain of corruption, every stream
that branches from it must partake of the foul-
ness of the source from whence it flows. Let
the failure of the past suffice to teach you, that
this holy law you can never keep. Let your
formal prayers, your lifeless religion, your vows
foresworn, your resolutions broken, all confirm
the solemn declaration of the Apostle—"by the
deeds of the law there shall no flesh be justified
in His sight." Again, "for by the law is the
knowledge of sin." Accompanied by the Spirit
of God, it discloses to the soul the sinfulness of
the heart and life. Convinces it of sin and
brings it in guilty and self condemned before
God. Now how is it possible that the law can
ever be an instrument of *life* and an instrument
of *death* to a sinner? It is utterly impossible
that it can be. It never yet gave spiritual life
to the soul,—It never yet emancipated the soul
from its thraldom—it never yet conducted it to
*Jesus*—it never yet whispered liberty and peace.

It can, and does, *condemn*, it can, and does, *curse*, and this is the utmost extent of its prerogative. O then, resign all the hope you fondly cherish of life, peace, and acceptance by "the deeds of the law," and betake yourself to Him who hath, by His most precious blood, "redeemed us from the curse of the law, being made a curse for us."

Having established the incapacity of the law to justify the sinner, the Apostle then proceeds to unfold the glory, fitness, and freeness of that righteousness which can and does justify the soul before GOD. He takes up and argues two important points :—The *nature* of the righteousness and the *instrument* by which it is received. With regard to the first, he declares it to be "the righteousness of GOD." Ver. 21, 22. As we have enlarged upon this point in another chapter, we dismiss it now with but one observation,—nothing but the "righteousness of GOD" can justify a soul in the sight of GOD. It must not be the righteousness of Angels, nor the righteousness of Adam, nor the righteousness of Moses—it must be the righteousness of GOD in our nature. Away with every other refuge— away with every other covering ; and let not the

reader dream of entering with acceptance into
the presence of a holy and a heart searching
GOD, clad in any other righteousness than that
which the adorable Immanuel wrought out. In
this righteousness the believing sinner is safe,
and safe forever. Take him for a moment out
of this righteousness, and he is lost, and lost
forever!

The *instrument* by which this Divine righteousness is received, is the second point established by this conclusive argument of the Apostle. He clearly proves it to be BY FAITH. Thus:
—"Even the righteousness of God which is *by
faith* of Jesus Christ unto all and upon all them
that *believe*." Ver. 22. And in ver. 25, "Whom
God hath set forth to be a propitiation *through
faith* in His blood." How perfectly does this
statement of the instrument or medium by which
the blessings of pardon and justification are received into the soul, harmonize with every other
portion of GOD's Word. Thus, for instance, "By
Him all that *believe* are justified from all things."
Acts, xiii. 39. "*Believe* in the Lord Jesus
Christ and thou shalt be saved." Acts, xvi. 31.
"*God so* loved the world that He gave His only

begotten son, that whosoever *believeth* in Him should not perish, but have everlasting life." John, iii. 16. "And as they went on their way, they came unto a certain water : and the eunuch said, See, here is water, what doth hinder me to be baptized? And Philip said, If thou *believest* with all thine heart, thou mayest. And he answered and said, I *believe* that Jesus Christ is the Son of God." Acts, viii. 36, 37. O see, disconsolate soul, the freeness of the gift—" To him that *believeth*," not to him that worketh—not to him that deserveth—not to the worthy, but "to him that *believeth*." " Where is boasting then ? It is excluded. By what law ? of works ? Nay: but by *the law of faith.* Therefore we conclude that a man is justified *by faith* (in Christ) without the deeds of the law."

Let not however, the subject of *faith* be misunderstood. Wrong views,—views contrary to God's Word, and inimical to the soul's spiritual peace, may be entertained by the seeker of salvation. There is a danger of giving to faith, precious and important as it is, undue prominence. We may *deify* faith. We may convert it into a *Saviour.* Substitute it for Christ, the great Ob-

*ject* of faith. Where this is the case, let not the seeking soul wonder that it finds not peace. Any thing, even if it be the blessed production of the Eternal Spirit of GOD, which takes the place of Christ, which shuts out Christ from the soul, is dangerous. In the great work of salvation, Christ must be every thing or nothing. From Him solely, from Him entirely, from Him exclusively must pardon and justification be drawn. Whatever then rises between the soul and Christ—whatever would tend to satisfy the soul in His absence—whatever would take His place in the affections, must be surrendered. Is it as the plucking out of a right eye? It must be yielded. Is it as the cutting off of a right hand? let it go. Christ in His Godhead, Christ in His humanity, Christ in His great and finished work, Christ in His mediatorial fulness, must be all in all to the sinner.

Now, this making a Christ of faith, this substituting of the *instrument* for the great Object, is the danger of which we caution the soul, seeking for salvation. On this point, we cannot be too earnest, or too explicit. The matter of a *sinner's* standing before GOD—the method of the soul's acceptance of Christ, are momentous themes. It is of the utmost importance that none should be satisfied with crude and obscure views. We say then that, faith is not the source of pardon and peace to the soul, but the mere instrument, the simple channel through which the Atonement, with its attendant blessings, is received by the repenting sinner. It is not the Saviour, but the instrument by which that Saviour is received. It is not the Fountain, but the channel through which that fountain flows. It is not the blood nor the righteousness of Christ, but the eye that looks at both. In itself, it possesses no intrinsic efficacy. It has no healing, peace imparting power. It is efficacious, it is healing, it is peace speaking as it leads, and only as it leads, the soul to Jesus, to His healing peace speaking blood. And what is that hanging back, that lingering, that waiting for more faith, for stronger faith, before the soul closes in with Christ,—what is it, but *making a Saviour of faith?* It is not great faith that saves the soul —It is not strong faith that pardons and justifies it. It is weak faith, small faith, "looking unto Jesus," as a rich, a full, an able and willing

*15**

Saviour. "So that the office of faith," in the words of an *old* Divine, "is to receive from, and not bring to Christ, unless it be wants and weakness, ill and hell deservings, sins without number, and obligations to punishments without end. Of all the graces of the Spirit, faith is the most emptying, accordingly goes empty, poor and indigent to Christ: Other graces bring something, as it were along with them; whereas faith brings nothing to Christ but a naked back. As in nature the hand and the mouth are both of them adapted to receive, the one a gift, the other food; so is faith adapted to look, to receive and to close with the Lord Jesus Christ; and, having received Him, to realize all those scripture motives, by which we are persuaded to abide with Him, and to follow Him: So that faith in the business of justification before GOD is not to be considered as a working, but as a receiving grace, through it is both, and sows in tears of godly sorrow, and works by love; but its first and great business is with the person and righteousness of Christ, particularly to receive the Atonement."

It is delightful to trace the different exhibitions

of faith which the Holy Ghost has presented to
our views in His own word. And He seems to
have thus spread them out before us, that the
ever varied and varying circumstances of the
saints of God, may be adequately met. In some
sections of His word, He has presented to our
views sturdy characters, impressed with the
lineaments of a strong, gigantic faith.

For example ;—That was strong faith in the
centurion, when he said, "Lord I am not worthy
that thou shouldest come under my roof: but
speak the word only, and my servant shall be
healed." Matt. viii. 8. That was great faith
exhibited in the case of the woman of Canaan,
who, at the apparent repulse of the blessed
Lord, would take no denial, but met His seeming objection, by saying, "Truth, Lord: yet the
dogs eat of the crumbs which fall from their
master's table. Then Jesus answered and said
unto her, O woman, great is thy faith: be it
unto thee even as thou wilt." Matt. xv. 27, 28.
That too was strong faith in Abraham, who
could take his son, his only son, his son whom
he loved, and offer him up at God's bidding.
And, to mention no more, that was strong, un-

wavering faith in Job, who could say, "though
He slay me, yet will I trust Him."

But on the other hand, the Holy Ghost presents to the view, some of the weakest exhibitions of faith, in order that no dear child of God,
reposing by simple reliance on Christ, might
despair. That was *feeble* faith which the leper
exercised when he said, "Lord if thou *wilt*, thou
canst make me clean." Matt. viii. 2. Here was
no doubting of Christ's *ability*—the only point
he seemed to question was, His *willingness* to
cleanse him. That was faith of the same feeble
character, exercised by the father who brought
his child possessed of a dumb spirit to Jesus, to
be dispossesed, with the request thus couched—
"If thou *canst* do any thing, have compassion on
us and help us." Mark, ix. 22. In this case,
Christ's *willingness* was fully believed, His
*ability* only doubted. And yet, in both cases,
the one that doubted His willingness, and the
other that doubted His ability, Christ manifested
His compassion, and answered their request.
Let no anxious, seeking, soul then, hang back
from Jesus, because of the weakness of its faith.
*It may* be small faith; it may be small in its de-

gree, and weak in its exhibition, yet it is "precious faith," yea, "like precious faith" with Abraham and Job, and all the Prophets and Apostles. If it be faith, however small, it yet is " the faith of GOD's elect," it is of the mighty operation of the Holy Ghost—and though feeble, yet, if it directs its eye out of, and off of itself, simply to Jesus, that single glance shall sweep the ocean fulness of His love in the soul. Only let the dear reader bear in mind that, *faith is not Christ, and can never be a substitute for Him.*

Pass now to the consideration of those kindred passages which declare the salvation of the sinner to be an act of mere GRACE. The reader will bear in mind our simple definition of *grace.* It means, GOD's unmerited favour to sinners. It implies no worthiness whatever in the creature. This is the glory of the gospel. " By *grace* are ye saved through faith; and that not of yourselves : it is the gift of GOD. Not of works lest any man should boast." Eph. ii. 8, 9. "Now to him that worketh—(O mark his expressions!) is the reward not reckoned of *grace,* but of debt. But to him that worketh not, but believeth *on* Him that justifieth the ungodly, his

faith is counted for righteousness." Rom. iv. 4, 5.
" Therefore it is of faith, that it might be by
*grace*." Ver. 16. " And if by *grace*, then is it
no more of works : otherwise grace is no more
grace. But if it be of works, then is it no more
grace : otherwise work is no more work." xi.
6. What language can possibly establish the
doctrine of the *freeness* of the Atonement more
conclusively than this? See the force of the
Apostle's argument. It lies here ;—if there be
ought of *merit* in the creature—if the works of
the sinner are the grounds, even partially so, on
which salvation is bestowed, then the reward, or
the blessing, is not a *free gift*, but the discharge
of a *debt*. A debt, let it be borne in mind, due
from GOD to the sinner! And in consequence of
his merit, in consequence of his works, pardon
and justification are thus made over to him!
What doctrine can be more awful than this?
what more opposed to GOD's Word? And yet,
the doctrine that teaches me, that I may present
myself before the Holy GOD with some *fitness*
of my own—some *price* in my hand, something
to *merit* GOD's forgivness, is this very doctrine!
*Survey* again the Apostle's argument ;—If there

be ought of merit in the creature—if it be so much as the raising of my hand, salvation is not of *grace*,—the Atonement is not *free*; and GOD —we tremble while we write it—GOD becomes the sinner's *debtor !*

The Atonement itself precludes all idea of human merit, and, from its *very nature*, proclaims that it is *free.* Consider the grandeur of the Atonement; contemplate its costliness. *Incarnate Deity—perfect obedience—spotless purity— unparalleled grace and love—acute and mysterious sufferings—wondrous death*—the *resurrection, ascension,* and *intercession* of the Saviour, all conspire to constitute it the most august sacrifice that could possibly be offered. And shall there be aught in the sinner to *merit* this sacrifice ? Shall GOD so lower its dignity, underrate its value, and dishonour Himself as to *barter* it to the sinner? And if GOD were so disposed, what is there in the sinner that could purchase it ? Where is the equivalent—where the price ? "Alas !" is the exclamation of a convinced soul, " I am a spiritual bankrupt—I lost every thing in my first parent who fell—I came into the world poor, and helpless—and to the sin of my nature, I have added actual transgression of the most aggravated character—I have nothing to recommend me to the favour of GOD—I have no claim upon His mercy—I have no price with which to purchase it, and if redemption is not free, without money, and without price, I am undone." The very *costliness* then, of the Atonement, puts it beyond all price, and stamps it with infinite freeness.

The great *source* of the Atonement stamps its *freeness*, What is that source? *The heart of* GOD! The Atonement, with all the blessings it involves, originated in the very heart of Jehovah. Where could the thought else have originated, of saving a guilty world, and saving it in such a way and at such a sacrifice? It was a stupendous thought,—even that of saving—of shewing mercy to rebellious man. The bare idea of exercising *love* towards the apostate race, was in itself so mighty, that, GOD alone could have conceived it. But when *the plan of salvation* is viewed—when the *method of mercy* is contemplated—when the sacrifice, " the price of pardon" is weighed,—that sacrifice, His only *begotten* and well beloved Son—that price, His

own most precious blood.—And O the grandeur of
the thought! Fitted only to have originated with
GOD, and in every view, worthy of Himself.
From what other and higher source then, could
the Atonement have proceeded if not from the
very *heart* of GOD? And from His heart it *did*
proceed. And not more freely does the sun
pour forth its streams of light, and not more
freely does the air fan with its refreshing influence, and not more freely does the ocean billow
heave, than the Atonement flows from the heart
of GOD! "God is love," and the seat of that love
is His heart. Towards a sinner standing in the
righteousness of His Son, that heart is love, all
love, and nothing but love. Not an unkind
thought lodging there. Not a repulsive feeling
dwelling there,—all is love, and love of the most
tender character. Yea, we dare affirm, that
towards His chosen people, there never has been,
and there never will be one thought of unkindness, of anger, of rebuke in the heart of GOD.
From eternity it has been love—through time it
is love, and on through eternity to come, it will
be love. "What! are not their afflictions, their
chastisements, the rough and thorny path they

16

tread proofs of GOD's displeasure? What! is
that individual loved of GOD whom I see yonder,
bearing that heavy and daily cross: against
whom billow after billow dashes—to whom,
messenger after messenger is sent, — whose
gourd's are withered in a night, and whose
fountains are all broken in a day,—whose person is diseased, whose domestic comforts are
fled,—who is poor, feeble and dependent: what!
is that individual beloved of GOD?"  Go and
ask that afflicted saint.  Go and ask that cross-
bearing disciple.  Go and ask that son and
daughter of disease, and penury—and they will
tell you;—their Father's dealings with them,
are the most costly proofs of His love.  That
instead of unkindness in that cross, there was
love—instead of harshness in that rebuke, there
was tenderness.  And that, when He withered
that gourd, and broke up that cistern, and removed that earthly prop, and blighted that bud-
ding hope, it was but to pour the tide of His
own love in the heart, and satiate the soul with
His goodness.  O dear cross! O sweet affliction! O precious discipline! thus to open the
heart of GOD; thus to unlock the treasury of His

love ; thus to bring God nigh to the soul, and the soul nigh to God. To return to the subject.

Let it not be forgotten that the Atonement had its origin in the *heart* of God. It follows then that it must be *free*. To recur again to our illustrations ;—Does the sun need bribing in order to shine ? Does the wind need persuasion in order to blow ? Does the ocean wave need argument in order to roll ? Is the sun-light purchased ? Is the air purchased ? Is the water that flows from the fountain purchased ? Not less *free* is the love of God, gushing from his *heart*, and flowing down through the channel of the cross of Christ, to a poor, repenting, believing sinner. *Without* works—*without* merit, *without* money, *without* price—without a previous fitness. *Convictions* do not merit it. *Repentances* do not merit it. *Tears* do not merit it. *Faith* does not merit it. Pardon to the chief of sinners ;—forgiveness to the vilest of the vile ;—the blotting out of sins of the deepest dye ;—the justification and acceptance of the most unworthy ;—all, *free* as the heart of God can make it. The hungry and the thirsty, the poor and the penniless, the weary and the heavy laden may come to the gospel provision, for the *heart* of GOD bids them welcome.

The OBJECTS contemplated in the special and gracious design of the Atonement, establishes its perfect *freeness* beyond all question. Who are they? Are they spoken of as the worthy, the righteous, the deserving, the rich, the noble? —The very reverse. They are *sinners*, *ungodly*, *unworthy*. Let the Holy Ghost speak;—"To him that worketh not, but believeth on Him that justifieth the UNGODLY, his faith is counted for righteousness." Rom, iv. 5. "When we were yet without strength, in due time Christ died for the UNGODLY." "GOD commendeth His love toward us, in that, while we were yet SINNERS, Christ died for us." V. 6, 8. And see how our blessed Lord confirms this statement. "I am not come to call the righteous" (that is, the self righteous—those who were righteousness in their own estimation, and despised others) but SINNERS to repentance." Matt. ix. 13. "The friend of publicans and sinners," was the charge these self-righteous, brought against Him. "This is a faithful saying, and worthy of all acceptation, *(O listen to* it reader, it is the declaration of one who styles himself the chief of sinners,) that Christ Jesus came into the world to save sinners: of whom I am chief." 1 Tim. i. 15.

And who did He save when upon earth? Were they the worthy or the most unworthy?—were they the righteous or sinners? Let us examine. Take the case of SAUL OF TARSUS. His own description of his previous character will certainly be believed. This it is—" which was before a blasphemer, and a persecutor, and injurious." And, in detailing before Agrippa the nature of his persecutions of the Christians, he says, " And I punished them oft in every synagogue, and compelled them to blaspheme; and being exceedingly mad against them, I persecuted them even unto strange cities." Acts xxvi. 11. And yet Saul of Tarsus "OBTAINED MERCY" —and why? He himself replies—" that in me first, Jesus Christ might shew forth all long suffering, FOR A PATTERN to them who should hereafter believe on Him to life everlasting." 1 Tim. i. 16. If Saul of Tarsus then, obtained mercy,—obtained it as a *sinner,* as a sinner of the deepest dye—obtained it fully, freely, aside from all human merit, penitent reader, so may you?

16*

It would expand beyond our intended limits, this volume, were we to adduce every prominent case of conversion recorded in the New Testament as illustrating the *freeness* of the Atonement. The reader is requested to open GOD's Word and turn to the cases of ZACCHEUS, the PHILIPPIAN JAILER—the WOMAN OF SAMARIA— MARY MAGDALENE, and the THIEF UPON THE CROSS. Let him examine minutely these several instances, and ascertain if there was aught of worthiness, of claim, of previous fitness, of price, in these individuals, wherefore they obtained mercy; but on the contrary, if they were not *ungodly—unrighteous, sinners,*—sinners of the most unworthy kind.

Let us attempt the application of this subject to the care of the *anxious, enquiring* reader, to whose eye this page may unfold itself. To such we observe,—

First ;—*The Atoning blood of Christ possesses a* PARDONING EFFICACY. We will suppose that you have been convinced of this cardinal truth, that GOD is *holy*, and from the very necessity of His nature, cannot but hate sin. Habak. i. 13. *We will* suppose too, that you have been brought

y the Eternal Spirit to the deep consciousness
f your utter sinfulness. That, convinced of
aving broken, and in breaking, of having in-
urred the penalty of GOD's holy law, you are
)oking wistfully around you for some effectual
emedy for the wound, some sure shelter from
ιe storm, some city of refuge to screen you from
ιe avenger of blood. O! then, what tidings
re here! Through this blood of Christ, GOD,
he holy GOD.—the GOD against whom you have
inned, and whose wrath you justly dread, can
ardon all your sins, blot out all your trans-
ressions, and take from you the terror of a guilty
onscience. O what news is this! Do you
oubt it? Do you look incredulous at the dec-
ιration of a truth so amazing? We know it is
n amazing fact, that GOD should pardon sin,
nd that He should pardon it too, through the
lood of His dear Son, yet take His own word as
 full confirmation of this stupendous fact, and
oubt no more,—"The blood of Jesus Christ
Iis Son, cleanseth us from all sin." 1 John, i.
.  O yes,—blessed declaration! it cleanseth
s from *all* sin—"all manner of sin"—We ask
ot *how heavy* the weight of guilt that rests upon

you—We ask not how wide the territory over
which your sins have extended—We enquire
not how many their number, or how aggravated
their nature, or how deep their dye—we meet
you, just as you are, with GOD's own declaration
—"the blood of Jesus Christ cleanseth us from all
sin." Many there are who can testify to this
truth. "Such were some of you," says the
Apostle, when writing to the Corinthian con-
verts, who had been fornicators, idolators, adul-
terers, effeminate, thieves, covetous, drunkards,
revilers, extortioners, "such were some of you,
but ye are washed." 1 Cor. vi. 9—11. In what
had they washed ?—where were they cleansed?
They washed in the "fountain opened to the
house of David and the inhabitants of Jerusalem
for sin and uncleanness." To this fountain they
came, guilty, vile, black as they were, and the
blood of Jesus Christ cleansed them from ALL
sin. Mourning soul, look up,—the Fountain yet
is open, and open too, for you. Satan will seek
to close it—unbelief will seek to close it—yet
it is ever running, ever overflowing, ever free—
Thousands have plunged in it, and emerged,
washed, sanctified and saved. To this Fountain

David, and Mannassah, and Saul, and Peter, and Mary Magdalene, and the dying Thief, and millions more, came, washed and were saved, and yet it has lost nought of its sin pardoning, sin cleansing efficacy;—full and free as ever! O, say not that you are too vile, say not that you are too unworthy. You may stand afar from its brink, looking at your unfitness, looking at your poverty, but listen while we declare that, led as you have been by the Holy Spirit to feel your vileness, for just such this precious blood was shed, this costly Fountain was opened.

We can tell you of one, who, in her deep sorrow for sin was brought to the extreme of mental anguish. Despairing of mercy, and anxious to anticipate the worst of her punishment, she resolved, when none should be near her, to terminate her life, and go, reeking with her own blood, to the bar of GOD. The fearful opportunity presented itself. The door was fastened, the knife prepared, and she fell on her knees to accomplish the awful deed. At the moment her hand was raised to give the fatal stroke, these words came to her mind with overwhelming *power*—"*the* blood of Jesus Christ His Son

cleanseth us from all sin." Her arm fell motion-
less at her side, the weapon dropped 'from her
convulsed grasp, and she exclaimed in a tran-
sport of relief, " If the blood of Christ Jesus
cleanseth from all sin, then why not *mine too* ?"
She arose—her fatal purpose was broken—her
perturbed spirit was calmed, and her heart drawn
out in prayer to God. On the following sabbath
she hastened to the house of God ; and to her
astonishment the minister announced as his text
—" the blood of Jesus Christ His Son, cleanseth
us from all sin." The Holy Spirit completed
the work so graciously begun in her soul—The
blood of Christ was applied to her conscience—
and from the terror and gloom of sin, she passe
into the sun shine of God's full and free forgiv
ness. Anxious soul, you too may come. W
not you ? True, you are unworthy, true, you
poor and penniless—so was this individual,
she " obtained mercy"—*and why not you ?*

Second ;—*It is peace speaking blood.* It
only *procured* peace, but, when applied by
Holy Spirit to the conscience, it *produces*
—it gives peace to the soul. It imparts a
of *reconciliation.* It removes all slavish

GOD, all dread of condemnation, and enables the soul to look up to GOD, not as "a consuming fire," but as a *reconciled* GOD—a GOD in covenant., Precious peace speaking blood, flowing from the "Prince of peace!". Applied to your heart penitent reader, riven assunder as it may be with godly sorrow, it shall be as a balm to the wound. Sprinkled on your conscience, burthened as it is with a sense of guilt, you shall have "beauty for ashes, the oil of joy for mourning, the garment of praise for the spirit of heaviness." It is peace speaking blood.

Third;—*It is through simply believing*, that the blood of Christ thus seals pardon and peace upon the conscience. Forget not this. "Only believe," is all that is required. And this faith is the free gift of GOD. And what is faith? It is "looking unto Jesus." It is simply going out of yourself and taking up your rest in the finished work of the Lord Jesus Christ. *This is faith.* Christ has said that, "whosoever cometh unto Him, He will in no wise cast out."—that "He saves to the uttermost all that come unto GOD by Him"—that He died for sinners, and that He saves sinners *as sinners* ; the Holy Spirit

working faith in the heart,—lifting the eye out
of, and off of the wound, and fixing it on the
Lamb of GOD, pardon and peace flow like a river
in the soul. O! stay not then from the gospel
feast, because you are poor, penniless and unworthy. Why starve and die, when there is
bread enough in your Father house, and to spare.
See the provision how full!—see the invitation
how free! see the guests, the poor, the maimed,
the lame, the blind! Come then to Jesus *just as
you are*. We stake our all on the assertion that,
He *will* welcome you, that He *will* save you.
There is too much efficacy in His blood, too
much compassion in His heart for poor sinners
—to reject you, suing at His feet for mercy.
Then look up, believer, and you shall be saved,
and all heaven will resound with hallelujahs
over a sinner saved by grace!

# CHAPTER V.

## THE SYMPATHY OF THE ATONEMENT.

### THE TRIED BELIEVER COMFORTED.

We have not an High Priest which cannot be touched with the
eling of our infirmities; but was in all points tempted like as we
e, yet without sin." Heb. iv. 15.

!OULD we draw aside, for a moment, the thin
eil that separates us from the glorified saints,
nd enquire of each, the path along which they
'ere conducted by a covenant GOD to their
resent enjoyments, how few exceptions, if any,
iould we find to that declaration of Jehovah, "I
ave chosen thee in the furnace of affliction."
sa. xlviii.10. Each would tell of some peculiar
ross—some domestic, relative or personal trial
'hich attended them every step of their journey,
-which made the vale they trod truly "a vale
f tears," and which they only threw off when
ie spirit, divested of its robe of flesh, fled where
orrow and sighing are forever done away.
*iod's people* are a sorrowful people. The first

17

step they take in the Divine life is connected
with tears of godly sorrow ; and as they travel
on, sorrow and tears do but track their steps.
They sorrow over the body of sin which they
are compelled to carry with them—they sorrow
over their perpetual proneness to depart, to back-
slide, to live below their high and holy calling.
They mourn that they mourn so little, they weep
that they weep so little ; that over to much indwelling sin, over so many and so great departures, they yet are found so seldom mourning
in the posture of one low in the dust before
GOD. In connexion with this, there is the
sorrow which results from the needed discipline
which the correcting hand of the Father who
loves them, almost daily employs. For, in what
light are all their afflictions to be viewed, but as
so many correctives, so much discipline em-
ployed by their GOD in covenant, in order to
make them "partakers of His holiness ?" Viewed
in any other light, GOD is dishonoured, the Spirit
is grieved, and the believer is robbed of the
great spiritual blessing for which the trial was
sent.

*There is* something so remarkable in the

words of the Holy Ghost which we have quoted that, before we enter more fully into the discussion of our subject, we must again call them to the reader's mind. The passage is, "I have chosen thee in the furnace of affliction." With what is the Divine will, as stated in these words, connected, respecting the afflictions of the believer? Is it with the circumstances of time?—Is it since they were brought into existence that GOD determined upon the circumstances that should surround them, and the path they should tread? O no! The trying circumstance, the heavy affliction stands connected with the great and glorious doctrine of GOD's eternal, sovereign and unconditional election of His people. They were "*chosen* in the furnace," chosen in it before all time—chosen in it from all eternity. Chosen in it, when He set His heart upon them,—entered into an everlasting covenant with them, and took them to be His " chosen generation, His royal priesthood, His holy nation, His peculiar people." O, thus to trace up every affliction that comes from GOD to His eternal choice of His people. To see it in the covenant of grace. To see it connected with His eternal purpose of salvation. Thus viewed in connexion with His *eternal love*, in what a soothing light does it place the darkest dispensation of His providence.

But, there is another thought in the passage, equally blessed. "I have chosen thee,"—in what? In prosperity? No—In the bright summer's day? No. In the smooth and flowery path of worldly comforts? No "I have chosen thee *in the furnace of affliction*."—"the furnace of affliction!"—Is this according to our poor finite ideas of love and tenderness? O no! Had we been left to choose our own path, to mark out our own way, it had been a far different one from this. We should never have thought of afflictions as a source of blessing. But God's thoughts are higher than our thoughts, and His ways above our ways.

Our great object in this work has been, to keep prominently and distinctly before the mind of the reader, the absolute necessity of *experimental* religion. Without this we have shewn that, all gifts and knowledge, and profession were worse than worthless. That if the grace of God be not in the heart, the truth of God merely settled in the understanding, as to all holy, practical

purposes, would avail a man nothing.  Having
expatiated upon the necessity and nature of experimental religion, together with the great Author of the work, it seems appropriate that the
reader now be led to a consideration of that
method which a good and covenant GOD frequently employs, yet further to deepen His gracious work in the heart of his dear child—to try
its character, test its genuineness, and bring the
soul more fully into a personal experience of the
truth.  This method it will be shown, is the *sanctified discipline of the covenant.*

The very *wisdom* seen in this method of instruction, proves its divine origin.  Had the
believer been left to form his own school, adopt
his own plan of instruction, choose his own discipline, and even select his own teacher, how
different would it have been from GOD's plan.
We should never have conceived the idea of
such a mode of instruction, so unlikely, according to our poor wisdom, to secure the end in
view.  We should have thought that, the smooth
path, the sunny path, the joyous path would the
soonest conduct us into the glories of the kingdom of grace—would more fully develope the

17*

wisdom, the love, the tenderness and sympathy
of our blessed Lord, and tend more decidedly to
our weanedness from the world, our crucifixion
of sin, and our spiritual and unreserved devotedness to his service. But, " my thoughts are not
your thoughts, neither are your ways my ways,
saith the Lord. For as the heavens are higher
than the earth, so are my ways higher than
your ways, and my thoughts than your thoughts."
Isa. lv. 8, 9.

Nor, is the believer fully convinced of the
wisdom of God's method of procedure, until he
has been brought, in a measure, *through* the
discipline. Until the rod has been removed, the
angry waves have subsided, and the tempest
cloud has passed away. Then, reviewing the
chastisement,—minutely examining its nature
and its causes,—the steps that led to it—the
chain of providences in which it formed a most
important link,—and most of all, surveying the
rich covenant blessings it brought with it—the
weanedness, the gentleness, the meekness, the
patience, the spirituality, the prayerfulness, the
love, the joy—he is led to exclaim, "I now see
the infinite *wisdom* and *tender mercy* of my

Father in this affliction. While in the furnace
I saw it not—the rising of inbred corruption,—
unbelief,—and hard thoughts of GOD darkened
my view, and veiled from the eye of my faith
the reason of the discipline—but *now* I see why
and wherefore my covenant GOD and Father
has dealt with me thus. I see the *wisdom*, and
adore the love of His merciful procedure." It
is our purpose to shew that, the path of affliction
along which the believer walks, is the path of
GOD's own appointment—and that, walking in
this path, he comes into the possession of rich
and varied blessings not found in any other.

This is a truth much forgotten, especially by
the young Christian, who has just set out on his
pilgrimage. To his eye, now opened to the
new world into which grace has introduced him
—all seems fair and lovely. "The love of his
espousals" is the one theme of his heart. All
above, beneath, and around him seems but the
image of his own joyous feelings. The sea unruffled, the skies unclouded, the vessel moving
gently as over a summer sea, and the haven of
rest full in view.

"Tongue cannot express,
The sweet comfort and peace,
Of a soul in its earliest love."

He thinks not that, all, now so fair, will soon
change. That the summer sea will be lashed
by angry billows,—that the sky will look dark
and threatening—that the fragile barque will be
tossed from billow to billow—and that the port
will be lost to sight. How needful then that
this important truth, *through much tribulation we
must enter the kingdom*, should be ever kept in
view.

In looking into GOD's Word, we find it full
and decisive on this point. We have already
commented upon Isa. xlviii. 10. "Behold I
have refined thee, but not with silver; I have
chosen thee in the furnace of affliction." There
is yet another remarkable declaration in Zech.
xiii. 9. "And I will bring the third part through
the fire, and will refine them as silver is refined,
and will try them as gold is tried." Our Lord's
own testimony harmonizes with this declaration.
"In the world *ye shall have tribulation*." As
though He had said, 'expect nothing less—it is
a world of sorrow, and while in it, ye shall have

tribulation. It is your lot. It is the way of my appointment—it is the path I have ordained you to walk in—it is the path I have trod myself, and I leave you an example that ye should follow my steps. In the world ye *shall* have tribulation but in me ye shall have peace.' And so taught His Apostles. They went forth, "confirming the souls of the disciples, and exhorting them to continue in the faith, and that we must *through much tribulation* enter into the kingdom of God." Acts, xiv. 22.

From the *declarations* of God's Word, let us pass to consider the *examples*. The entire histories of the Old and New Testament saint's present to us a people "chosen in the furnace of affliction." Paul enquires, "what son is there whom the Father chasteneth not?" He seems to throw out a challenge—'where is the exception to this principle of the Divine procedure? Where is the child taken into God's family, where is the adopted son who has never felt the smartings of the rod,—whom the father chasteneth not?' More than this.—Let it not be supposed that the feeblest of God's saints,—those who have the least measure of grace and strength, who find the ascent difficult, and whose advance is slow and tardy, are those whom the Lord most frequently and sharply afflicts. O no! In looking into the Word of truth—in reading the memoirs of GOD's ancient saints, it will be found that, those whom He blessed most,—who were the most distinguished for some eminent grace of the Spirit, some mighty exploit of faith, some great act of devotedness, were those whom He *most deeply afflicted.* "The branch that beareth fruit, he purgeth it that it may bring forth more fruit."—Let the histories of Abraham, Jacob, Moses, Job and David testify. Let Paul's thorn in the flesh speak. And what is the testimony? *that, the most eminent of GOD's saints are the most afflicted.* Their eminence grew out of their afflictions. Like their blessed Lord, they were perfected through suffering. They became thus strong in faith, holy in life, close in their walk, devoted in the service of their Master, by the very discipline through which they passed. They were eminently holy, because eminently tried.

And what was the life of our adorable Lord? *Any thing* but exemption from suffering. His

life was one continuous trial. From the moment
He entered our world He became leagued with
suffering. He identified Himself with it in its
almost endless forms. He seemed to have been
born with a tear in His eye, with a shade of
sadness on His brow. He was prophesied as
"a man of sorrows, and acquainted with grief."
And, from the moment He touched the horizon
of our earth, from that moment His sufferings
commenced. Not a smile lighted up His benign
countenance from the time of His advent to His
departure. He came not to indulge in a life of
tranquillity and repose. He came not to quaff
the cup of earthly or of Divine sweets—for even
this last was denied Him in the hour of His
lingering agony on the cross. He came to suffer.
He came to bear the curse. He came to drain
the deep cup of wrath, to weep, to bleed, to die.
Our Saviour was a *cross bearing* Saviour. Our
Lord was a *suffering* Lord. And was it to be
expected that they who had linked their destinies
with His—who had avowed themselves His
disciples and followers, should walk in a path
diverse from their Lord's? He Himself speaks
of the *incongruity* of such a division of interests

—"The disciple is not above his master, nor the servant above his lord. It is enough for the disciple that he be as his master, and the servant as his lord." Matt. x. 24, 25. There can be no true following of Christ as our *example*, if we lose sight of Him as a *suffering* Christ—an *afflicted* Saviour. There must be fellowship with Him in His sufferings. In order to enter fully and sympathetically into the afflictions of His people, He stooped to a body of suffering —in like manner, in order to have sympathy with Christ in His sorrows, we must in some degree, tread the path He trod. Here is one reason, why He ordained that, along this rugged path His saints should all journey. They must be like their Lord. They are one with Him. And this oneness can only exist where there is mutual sympathy. The church must be a *cross bearing* church. It must be an *afflicted* church. Its great and glorious Head, sought not and found not repose here. This was not His rest. He turned His back upon the pleasures, the riches, the luxuries and even the common comforts of this world, preferring a life of obscurity, penury and suffering. His very submission seemed to impart dignity to suffering, elevation to poverty, and to invest with an air of holy sanctity, a life of obscurity, want, and trial.

We are far from considering the *present posture* of the church, that of a cross bearing church. The church has thrown off the cross. Her path would be less smooth, the world less her friend, and she less the favourite of the world, were this not the case. How can we believe that she is bearing the cross, when we view her trimming policy, her compromising character, her worldly conformity, her efforts to catch the vain breath of human applause, her self proclaimed importance, her heralded benevolence, her trumpeted fame, her sectarian badge—the waving of her treason flag, and the shout of her shibboleth?—O no! She bears not the cross as in her primitive days. We speak not in a tone of unkind rebuke. We love the church universal. We love all, and know no distinction of name or sect—who love the Lord Jesus in sincerity and in truth. And it is this love we bear the whole elect of God, which impels us to avow our solemn conviction that, the *present* is not the *cross bearing age* of the church. True,

18

she is extending her conquests far and wide:
True, she is sending the preached and the oral
word into almost every accessible part of the
globe.   True, she is pouring in of her abundance
into the treasury of the Lord.—Yet with all this
seeming prosperity, the true piety of the church
may be exceedingly low, and there may exist in
her bosom evils, that call loudly for the correcting hand of God.

We have seen then, that our blessed Lord
sanctified, by His own submission, a life of suffering.   And that all His followers, if they would
resemble Him, must have fellowship with Him
in His sufferings.   The Apostle Paul seems to
regard this in the light of a *privilege*.   "For
unto you," he says, "it is *given* in behalf of
Christ, not only to believe on Him, *but also to
suffer for His sake.*"  Philipp. i. 29.   It seems
too, to be regarded as a part of their *calling*.
"For even hereunto *were ye called*: because
Christ also suffered for us, *leaving us an example, that ye should follow His steps.*"  1 Pet. ii. 21.
Happy will be that afflicted child of God, who
is led to view his Father's discipline in the light
of a *privilege*.   To drink of the cup that

Christ drank of—To bear any part of the cross
that He bore. To tread in any measure the
path that He trod, is a privilege indeed. This
is a distinction which angels have never attained.
They know not the honour of suffering with
Christ, of being made conformable to His death.
It is peculiar to the believer in Jesus. It is his
*privilege*, his *calling*.

There is often a *severity*, a *grievousness* in the
chastisements of our covenant GOD, which it is
important and essential to the end for which it
was sent, not to overlook. "Now no chastisement for the present seemeth to be joyous but
*grievous*." Heb. xii. 2. He who sent the chastisement appointed its character. He intended
that *it should be felt*. There is, we would solemnly remind the reader, as much danger in
*underrating* as in *overrating* the chastisements of
GOD. It is not uncommon to hear some of
GOD's saints remark, in the very midst of His
dealings with them, "I feel it to be no cross at
all. I do not feel it an affliction. I am not
conscious of any peculiar burthen." Is it not
painful to hear such expressions from the lips of
a *dear child of* GOD? It betrays a want, so to

speak, of *spiritual sensitiveness*—a deficiency of
that tender, acute feeling which ought ever to
belong to him who professes to have reposed on
Jesus's bosom.  Now we solemnly believe that,
it is the Lord's holy will that His child should *feel*
the chastisement to be grievous.  That the smartings of the rod should be felt.  Moses, Jacob,
Job, David, Paul, all were made to exclaim,
"The Lord hath chastened me sore."

There are many *considerations* which seem to
add a grievousness to the chastisements of God.
When it is remembered that our chastisements
often *grow out of our sin.*  That, to subdue
some strong indwelling corruption, or, to correct
for some outward departure, the rod is sent.
This should ever humble the soul,  This should
ever cause the rebuke to be rightly viewed.  That,
were it not for some strong indwelling corruption,
or some step taken in departure from God, the
affliction would have been withheld,  O how
should every stroke of the rod lay the soul in
the dust before God.  "If God had not seen sin
in my heart, and sin in my outward conduct, He
would not have dealt thus heavily with me."
*And* were the *grievousness* of the chastisement

is not *felt*, is there not reason to suspect that the *cause* of the chastisement has not been discovered and mourned over ?

There is the consideration too, that the stroke *comes from the Father who loves us,*—loves us so well that, if the chastisement were not needed, there would not be a feather's weight laid on the heart of His child. Dear to Him as the apple of His eye, would He inflict those strokes if there were not an absolute necessity for them? "What! is it the Father who loves me that now afflicts me ? Does this stroke come from His heart ? What! does my Father see all this necessity for this grievous chastening ? Does He discover in me so much evil, so much perverseness, so much that He hates and that grieves Him, that this severe discipline is sent?" O how does this thought, that the chastisement proceeds from the Father who loves him, impart a keenness to the stroke.

And then there is often something *in the very nature* of the chastisement itself that causes its grievousness to be felt. The wound may be in the tenderest part. The rebuke may come through some idol of the heart. God may con-

18*

vert some of our choicest blessings into sources
of the keenest sorrow. How often does He, in
the wisdom and sovereignty of His dealings,
adopt this method. Abraham's most valued blessing became the cause of his acutest sorrow.
The chastisement may come through the beloved
*Isaac.* The very mercy we clasp to our warm
hearts so fondly, may be GOD's voice to us,
speaking in the tone of severe yet tender rebuke.
Samuel, dear to the heart of Eli, was GOD's solemn voice to His erring yet beloved servant.

Let no afflicted believer then, think lightly of
his chastisements. It is the Lord's will that he
should feel them. They were sent for this purpose. If I did not feel the cross ;—if I was not
conscious of the burthen, if the wound were not
painful, I should never take it to the mercy seat,
there to seek all needed grace, support and
strength. The burthen must first be *felt* before
it is cast upon the Lord. The chastisement
must be felt to be *grievous*, before the tenderness
and sympathy of Jesus will be sought.

There is equal danger of *overrating* our afflictions. When they are allowed to too deeply to
absorb us in grief. When they unfit us for duty

—keep us from walking in the path GOD has marked out for us—hold us back from prayer and from the means of grace,—when they lead us to think hardly, and speak harshly of GOD, *then* we overrate GOD's chastisements, and prevent the good they were so kindly sent to convey.  There are many and rich *blessings* found in this, the Lord's appointed path of affliction, and in no other, which we would for a moment glance at. We speak now of those afflictions which have been *sanctified* to the soul by the Spirit of GOD.

First,—*The view they give us of the faithfulness of GOD in sending the affliction, is no small mercy.*  This was the light in which David viewed his afflictions.  "I know O Lord, that thy judgments are right, and that thou *in faithfulness* hath afflicted me."  Ps. cxix. 75.  O what an act and triumph of faith is this, to count GOD *faithful* in sending the affliction.  When —messenger follows messenger—when wave follows wave—when our dearest comforts are taken—our cisterns broken—our props removed from beneath us—children, friends, health, wealth, character, all, touched by GOD, O, *then* to feel and acknowledge that, GOD is *faithful*,

still—that, "in *faithfulness* He hath afflicted".
It is one thing to be convinced in the judgment
of this truth, and it is another thing to acknowledge and approve of it in the heart. But, when
the Eternal Spirit works in the tried believer
this still, composed and satisfied frame, *then* the
language of the bereaved and wounded, yet re-
signed heart is, "True, Lord, I needed this rod,
my heart was torped, wavering, wandering, proud.
This rouses, fixes, recalls, humbles me. I know
thee, love thee better now. I see the emptiness
of self and the world, and I die to both. Thou
Lord, wilt have my *whole* heart, Lord it is thine.
Thy love is judicious, not falsely fond. It is in
*faithfulness* to my soul that thou hast afflicted.
My *good*, not my *ease*, is what thou, My God
and Father consulteth. It is *good* for me that I
have been afflicted."

It is no small attainment, to be built up in the
*faithfulness* of God. This forms a stable foundation of comfort for the believing soul. Mu-
tability marks every thing out of God. Look
into the church, into the world, into our families,
our selves, what innumerable changes do we see
on every hand. A week, one short day, what

alterations does it produce. Yet, in the midst
of it all, to repose calmly on the unchangeableness, the faithfulness of GOD. To know that,
no alterations of time—no earthly changes, effect
His faithfulness to His people. And more than
this,—no changes in them,—no unfaithfulness
of theirs, causes the slightest change in GOD.
Once a Father, ever a Father. Once a Friend,
ever a Friend. His providences may change,
His heart cannot. He is a GOD of unchangable
love. The promise He has given He will ful-
fil. The covenant He has made, He will observe. The word that has gone out of His mouth
He will not alter. "He cannot deny Himself."
Peace then, tried believer! Are you passing
*now*, through the deep waters? who kept you
from sinking when wading through the *last?*
Who brought you through the *last* fire? Who
supported you under the *last* cross? Who delivered you out of the *last* temptation? Was it
not GOD, thy covenant GOD—thy faithful unchangeable GOD? This GOD then, is your GOD
now, and your GOD forever and ever, and He
will be your guide even unto death. It is walk-

ing in the ordained path of trial that, the believer learns out the Divine faithfulness.

In this path too, he learns ` *his own nothingness.* And what a lesson is this to acquire! For a child of GOD, not to confess merely,—for nothing is easier than confession, but to *feel* his nothingness—to be conscious that he is the "least of all saints." To be willing to be thought so. To feel no repining at being overlooked—cast in the shade—yea, trampled under foot—O what an attainment is this! And yet, how few reach it : How few aspire after it. It is to be learned only in the path of *sanctified affliction.* Other discipline may mortify, but not humble the pride of the heart—It may wound, but not crucify it. Affliction, sanctified by the Spirit of GOD, lays the soul in the dust. Gives it low thoughts of itself. Gifts, attainments, successful labours, the applause of men, all, conspire the ruin of a child of GOD. And, but for the prompt, and often severe, discipline of an ever watchful, ever faithful GOD, would accomplish their end. But the affliction comes—the needed cross—the required medicine,—and in this way are brought out "the peaceable fruits of righteousness"—the most beautiful and precious of which is, *a humble, lowly view of self.*

And is not this too the method by which *holiness* is attained? So says GOD's own word. Speaking of the needed chastisements of our heavenly Father, the Apostle assures us that, they were for "our profit, that we might be *partakers of His holiness."* Heb. xii. 10. Job anticipated this as the result of GOD's afflictive dealings with him, "When he hath tried me, I shall come forth as gold." Job, xxiii. 10. It is the fire of affliction—the furnace of trial, that *searches* and *purifies* the heart. It is here the tin and the tinsil are consumed. It is here the dross is separated from the pure ore, and the gold is brought forth reflecting back the image of Him who, as the Refiner, watches with tenderness, and faithfulness, the process of trial through which the precious metal is passing.

And, is not this the method by which *the righteousness of Christ* is made to stand out in all its glory and fitness? Sanctified affliction teaches the soul its utter destitution. The believer often commences his spiritual journey, with shallow and defective views of the perfect

fitness and glory of the Redeemer's justifying
righteousness.    There is, we admit, a degree of
self renunciation—there is a reception of Christ
—and there is some sweet and blessed enjoyment
of his acceptance.  Yet, his views of himself, and
of the entire, absolute, supreme necessity, importance and glory of Christ's finished work, are
as nothing compared with his *after* experience
of both.    God will have the righteousness of
His Son to be acknowledged and felt to be every-
thing.    It is a great work, a glorious work, a
finished work, and He will cause His saints to
know it.    It is His *only* method of saving sinners; and the sinner that is saved, shall acknowledge this, not in his judgment merely, but
from a deep heart felt experience of the truth,
'*to* the praise of the glory of His grace.'
    It is then, we say, in the successive stages of
his experience, that the believer sees more distinctly, and adores more profoundly, and grasps
more firmly, the finished righteousness of Christ.
And what is the school in which he learns his
nothingness, his poverty, his utter destitution?
*the school of deep and sanctified affliction.*    In no
other school is it learned, and under no other

teacher but GOD. Here his high thoughts are brought low, and the Lord alone is exalted. Here he forms a just estimate of his attainments, his gifts, his knowledge—and that which he thought to be so valuable he now finds to be nothing worth. Here, his proud spirit is abased, his rebellious spirit tamed, his restless, feverish spirit soothed into passive quietude, and here, the deep, humbling acknowledgment is made, "I am vile!" Thus is he led back to first principles. Thus, the first step is retaken, and the first lesson is relearned. The believer, emptied entirely of self, of self complacency, self trust, self glorying, stands ready for the *full Saviour*. The blessed and Eternal Spirit opens to him, in this posture, the fitness, the fulness, the glory, the infinite grandeur of Christ's finished righteousness. Leads him to it afresh—puts it upon him anew—causes him to enter into it more fully,—to rest upon it more entirely. Breaks it up to the soul—and discloses its perfect fitness to his case. And what a glory he sees in it! He saw it before, but not as he beholds it *now*. And what a resting place he finds beneath the cross! *He rested there before, but not as he*

rests *now*. Such views has he now of Christ,—
such preciousness, such beauty, such tenderness
he sees in Immanuel—that, a new world of
beauty and of glory seems to have floated before
his view. A *new* Saviour, a *new* righteousness appear to have been brought to his soul.
All this has been produced by the discipline
of the covenant—the afflictions sent and sanctified by a good and covenant GOD and Father.
O ye tried believers! murmer not at GOD's dispensations. Repine not at His dealings. Has
He seen fit to dash against you billow upon billow? Has He thought proper to place you in
the furnace? Has He blasted the fair prospect
—dried up the stream—called for the surrender
of your Isaac? O *bless* Him for the way He
takes to empty you of self, and fill you with His
own love. This is His method of teaching you,
schooling you, and meetening you for the inhe-
ritance of the saints in light. Will you not
allow Him to select his own plan—to adopt His
own mode of cure? You are in His hands, and
could you be in better? Are you now learning
your own poverty, destitution and helplessness?
and is the blood and righteousness of Jesus more
*precious* and glorious to the eye of your faith?

Then *praise* Him for your afflictions—for all these cross dispensations are now, yea at this moment, working together for your spiritual good. It is no small mercy to have clear, close views of the glory and absolute fitness of Christ's righteousness. "If from this moment," is the beautiful sentiment of an old divine, "I had all the purity of angels, all the sanctity of seraphs, all the immaculate love of pure spirits made perfect, I would part with all to stand before GOD in the righteousness of Christ." Other, and equally important blessings might be enumerated as resulting from the sanctified dealings of GOD with His people. Leaving the tried and experienced reader to supply them from a page of his own history, we pass to the consideration of the SYMPATHY OF CHRIST, as the point to which we had intened to have given more distinct prominency in this chapter.

The view which the Atonement presents of the sympathy of Christ is most glorious. The Divine compassion and sympathy could only be revealed by the *incarnation* of Deity. In order to the just exhibition of sympathy of one individual with another, there must be a similarity *of circumstances.* The like body must be inhabited, the same path must be trod, the same, or a similar sorrow must be felt. There can be no true sympathy apart from this. A similarity of circumstances is indispensably necessary. See then the *fitness* of Christ to this very purpose. GOD took upon Him our nature, *in order* to bear our griefs, and carry our sorrows. Here we enter into the blessedness that flows from the human nature of Christ, As GOD merely, He could not endure suffering, nor weep, nor die. As *man* only, He could not have sustained the weight of our sin, grief, nor sorrow. There must be a union of the two natures to accomplish the two objects, in one person. The Godhead must be united to the manhood. The one to obey, the other to die. The one to satisfy Divine justice, the other to sympathize with the people in whose behalf the satisfaction was made. Let not the Christian reader shrink from a full, and distinct recognition of the doctrine of our Lord's humanity. Let it be an important article of his creed, as it an essential pillar of his hope. If the Deity of Jesus is precious, so is His humanity. The one is of no avail in the work of redemption apart from the other. It is the blending of the two in mysterious union that constitutes the "great mystery of godliness."

Approach then, the humanity of your adorable Lord. Turn not from it. It was pure humanity. It was not the form of an angel He assumed. Nor did He pause, in His descent to our world, to attach Himself to an order of intelligent being, if such there be, existing between the angelic and the human. It was pure humanity—bone of our bone and flesh of our flesh, which He took up into intimate and indissoluble union with His Deity. It was humanity too, in its *suffering* form. Our Lord attached Himself to the woes of our nature. He indentified Himself with sorrow in its every aspect. This was no small evidence of the love and condescension of Jesus. To have assumed our nature, this had been a mighty stoop.—But, to have assumed its most humiliating, abject form, this surpasses all our thoughts of His love to man. The dark picture of fallen humanity was before Him, drawn in its most gloomy and repulsive features—and, although He could not possibly have taken up into

19*

union with Him our fallen humanity, without the peculiar weakness inseparable from it, yet, there were walks through life He might have chosen, and in which suffering and sorrow would have been greatly mitigated and softened, if not entirely unknown. But, He choose the *suffering* state—He preferred to link Himself with sorrow and tears, they being more in harmony with the mission on which He had come, and with His own pensive and sympathetic nature.

It was necessary that our Lord, in order to sympathize fully with His people, should not only identify Himself with their *nature*, but in some degree, with their peculiar *circumstances*. This He did. It is the consolation of the believer to know that, the Shepherd has gone *before* the flock. He bids them not walk in a path which His own feet have not first trod, and left their impress. As the dear, tender, ever watchful Shepherd of His sheep, He "goeth before them," and it is the characteristic of His sheep that, they "follow Him." Our Lord was eminently fitted to enter sympathetically into every circumstance of his dear family, so that, no believer shall be able to say—"mine is a solitary case—my path is a lonely path—I walk where there are no foot prints—I bear a cross which none have borne before me—Surely Jesus cannot enter sympathetically into my circumstances." Then there were an end to the tender sympathy of Christ. If there were a case among His dear family, of trial, affliction or temptation in which Jesus could not enter, then He could not be "in all points" the merciful and sympathetic High Priest. View the subject in any aspect, and ascertain if Jesus is not fitted for the peculiarity of that case. Shall we commence with the *finer* feelings of our nature? they belonged to Him, and in Him, were of a far more exquisitely tender and chastened character than in us. His heart was delicately attuned to the gentlest harmony of ours. Not a refined and tender emotion, but He possessed in a higher order—The tenderest affection, the most delicate and confiding friendship were not strangers to His capacious heart. He knew too, what it was to have those gentle ties rudely sundered by inconstancy, or painfully severed by death. Over the treachery of one and the tomb of another, His sensative spirit had poured out its grief. Beloved reader, the heart of Jesus is composed of the finest chords. You know not how accurately and delicately it is attuned to yours—whether the chord vibrates in a joyous or a sorrowful note. You are perhaps walking in a solitary path. There is a peculiarity in your trial—It is of a nature so delicate that, you shrink from disclosing it even to your dearest earthly friend; and though surrounded by human sympathy, yet there is a friend you still want, to whom you can disclose the feelings of your bosom—*That friend is Jesus.* There is sympathy in Jesus to meet your case. Go to Him—open all your heart—be not afraid,—He invites, He bids you come.

Christian reader, we suppose you to be no stranger to grief. Your heart has known what sorrow is. You have borne perhaps for years some heavy, painful, yet concealed cross. Over it, in the solitude and silence of privacy, you have wept, agonized and prayed. And still the cross, though mitigated, is not removed. Have you ever thought of the sympathy of Christ? Have you ever thought of Him *as bearing that cross with you?* As entering into its peculiarity, its minutest circumstance? O, there is a fibre in His

heart that sympathizes, there is a chord there
that vibrates to that grief of yours. It is touched, the moment sadness and sorrow find their
lodgment in your bosom. *That cross* He is
bearing with you at this moment. And although
you may feel it to be so heavy and painful as to
be lost to the sweet consciousness of this, still,
it rests on Him, as on you, and where He to remove His shoulder but for a moment, you would
be crushed beneath its pressure. " Then why,
if so tender and sympathizing, does He place
upon me this cross ?" *Because of His tenderness and sympathy.* He sees you need that
cross. You have carried it, it may be, for years ;
who can tell where, and what, you would have
been at this moment, but for this very cross ?
What evil in you it may have checked—what
corruption in you it may have subdued—what
constitutional infirmities it may have weakened
—from what lengths it has kept you, from what
rocks and precipices it has guarded you—and
what good it has been silently and secretly, yet
effectually, working in you all the long years of
your life—who can tell but God Himself ? The
removal of that cross, might have been the re-

moval of your greatest mercy. Hush then, every murmer—be still and know that He is God, and that, all these trials, these cross dispensations, these untoward circumstances are *now* working together for your good and His glory.

And what would you know,—may we not ask,—of Jesus,—His tenderness, and love, and sympathizing heart, but for the rough and thorny path along which you have thus been led? The glory and fulness, the preciousness and sympathy of Christ, are not learned in every circumstance of life. The hour of prosperity, when every thing passes smoothly on, providences smiling—the heart's surface unruffled—the bud of hope expanded into the full flower—the gladsome sun light of creature happiness gilding every prospect with its brightness—this is not the hour, nor these the circumstances most favourable to an experimental acquaintance with Christ. It is in the dark hour—the hour of trial and of adversity—when the sea is rough and the sky is lowering, and providences are mysterious, and the heart is agitated, and hope is disappointed,—its bud nipped, and its stem broken, and creature comfort and support fail—O, then it is, the fulness and preciousness and tenderness of Jesus are learned. Then it is the heart loosens its hold on created objects, and entwines itself more fondly and more closely around the incarnate Son of GOD. Blessed Jesus! thou Brother born for our every adversity! didst thou take our nature up into union with thine own? And canst thou, dost thou weep when we weep, and rejoice when we rejoice? O thou adorable Son of GOD! we stand amazed, and are lost in this love, this condescension and this sympathy of thine. Draw our hearts to thyself—Let our affections rise and meet in thee, their centre, and cling to thee, their all.

Shall we go on, as we proposed, to classify the peculiar trying circumstances of GOD's dear family? They are so many and so diversified, we know not where to commence, nor where to terminate. "Many are the afflictions of the righteous." Each heart has its own sorrow— each soul bears its own cross. But Jesus is enough for all. He has sympathy for each and all His suffering people. Are you suffering from *pining sickness*?—Are your days wearisome and your nights sleepless, from the inroads of disease? Then, there is sympathy in Christ for you—for it is written, "Himself took our infirmities, and bore our sicknesses." He remembereth that you are but dust—and we doubt not, His blessed body knew what languid days and sleepless nights were. O, then, think of Jesus. That disease that wastes you—that pain that racks you—that debility that swoons you, Jesus knows fully and sympathetically. True He is now beyond all physical feelings—yet His tender heart sympathizes still.

Are you suffering from *temporal poverty?* Are sources on which you depended broken up? Friends on whom you leaned, removed? Does want stare you in the face? And are you at a loss to know from whence the next supply may come? Even *here* my brother, even *here* my sister, can Jesus sympathize with you. He, like you, and like the greater part of His people, was *poor* in this world's goods. No home sheltered, no daily spread table provided for Him. He was a poor—homeless, houseless, friendless wanderer. The foxes had holes, and the birds had nests, but Jesus had not where to lay His blessed head—that head that ached and bled for you. Take your poverty to Him—take your wants to Him. Let the principle of *faith* now be exercised. Has He died for your soul—has He pardoned your sins—Has He given you Himself, then will He not, with Himself, freely give you all things necessary for your temporal comfort while yet a pilgrim upon earth? Take your poverty and your want simply and directly to Jesus—Think it not too mean and too trivial to disclose to Him—He has an *ear* to hear your cry, an *heart* to sympathize with your case, and a *hand* to supply all your need. Then again we say, *take your wants simply and directly to Christ.*

Has *death* entered your domestic circle, plucking from it some precious and valued member? the affectionate parent—the tender husband—the fond wife, or the engaging child—has he "put lover and friend far from you," leaving the heart to weep in silence and sadness over the wreck of hopes that were so bright, and over the rupture of ties that were so tender?—O, there is sympathy in Christ even for this. Jesus knew what it was to weep over the grave of buried love—of friendship interred—He

20

knew what it was to have affection's ties broken
—leaving the heart wounded and bleeding.   He
can enter into your sorrow, bereaved reader.
Yes, even into *yours*.   See Him at the tomb of
Lazarus.   See Him weep—"behold how He
loved him"—what! do you repair to the grave of
the dear departed one to weep, and Jesus not
sympathize with you?   Let not unbelief close up
this last, remaining source of consolation—the
tender sympathy of Christ.   He can enter into
those tears of yours—the heart's desolateness,
loneliness and disappointment, are not unknown
and unnoticed by our blessed Immanuel.   And
why has the Lord dealt with you thus? why
has He torn the idol from its temple?—why
has He emptied the heart, and left it thus lonely
and desolate?  O why, but to prepare that temple
for Himself—why, but to pour into its emptiness
the full tide of His own precious love, and sympathy.   For this, beloved, has He been, and it
may be, is *now* dealing with you.   *That heart
belongs to Him*,—He bought it at a costly price;
—*It belongs to Him*,—He vanquished it by the
Omnipotence of His Spirit.   *It belongs to Him*,
—He has sealed it with His precious blood.

And He would have you know this too, by deep and sweet *experience.* He would have you know *how* He has loved you, and loves you still —He would have you know that, you are His— His by eternal election—His by gift—by purchase—by conquest—by a covenant that all your departures, all your unfaithfulness, all your unworthiness, all the changing scenes through which you pass, shall never and can never alter. All this, it is His will you should *experience.* Then, bow with submission to the discipline; as a weaned child, sit you at His feet, adopting His own blessed words—"Not my will but thine be done."

Thus, dear reader, does the glorious Atonement of the Son of GOD, open to us the ocean *sympathy* of His heart. But for that Atonement, nothing should we have known of His sympathy —but for His cross, nothing of His love—but for His death, nothing of joy on earth, and nothing of glory in heaven. All, all springs from the ATONEMENT of Jesus. "Seeing then that we have a great High Priest, that is passed into the heavens, Jesus the Son of GOD, let us hold fast our profession. For we have not an High

Priest which cannot be touched with the feeling of our infirmities; but was in all points tempted like as we are, yet without sin. Let us therefore come boldly unto the throne of grace, that we may obtain mercy, and find grace to help in time of need." Heb. iv. 14—16.

> "Soon we go from grace to glory,
> God's own hand shall lead us there;
> Soon shall we rehearse the story
> Of His gracious dealings here.
>
> Soon will end our earthly mission,
> Soon will pass our pilgrim days,
> Hope give place to full fruition,
> Faith to sight, and prayer to praise."

# CHAPTER VI.

## THE FEARFUL ALTERNATIVE OF REJECTING
## THE ATONEMENT.

### THE IMPENITENT SINNER WARNED.

"There remaineth no more sacrifice for sins, but a certain fearful
looking for of judgment and fiery indignation which shall devour the
adversaries." Heb. x. 26,27.

MANY will doubtless be induced, from various
motives, to read these humble pages, who will
assent and consent to the truths it discusses, the
doctrine it advocates, and even the one principle
on which it constantly insists—viz. The necessity of experimental religion—and yet shall close
it and retire, thinking as lightly of the great
Atonement of the Son of GOD as the child of the
diamond with which it for a moment toys, then
crushes as a thing of no value, beneath its feet.
There is such a thing, my impenitent reader, as
assenting to the great Atonement of Christ, de-
fending ably and successfully its Divine char-

acter, its expiatory nature and its definite design, and yet living without its practical influence upon the mind, the affections and the life ; and dying, as fearfully rejecting it and with equal guilt, as he, who openly avowed his disbelief in the Divine revelation of the doctrine. There may be a secret, practical rejection of the atoning blood, while the judgment fully and cordially assents to its truth and its necessity.—It is not he who merely yields an intellectual assent to the truth of GOD's word, who is accepted of GOD. Something far beyond this is needed. The Atonement is a practical, influential, life imparting and life sustaining principle. It demands more than the bare and cold assent of the judgment. The *heart* must welcome it, and in order thus to welcome it, that heart must have mourned over the bitterness of sin and in deep and unfeigned repentance before a holy GOD. Again we assert it, and, would that the sentiment were carried to the conscience of the reader and fastened there by the Eternal Spirit of GOD—no man shall value the precious blood of Christ, until he has been made to see and feel himself *to be a lost* and undone sinner. Christ is pre-

cious only to the soul that feels its spiritual
poverty, its vileness, its emptiness, its nothingness—To such an individual, Jesus is every
thing.  The deeper the Eternal Spirit leads him
to an acquaintance with himself, the more precious is that Saviour, whom he now finds to be
the very Saviour that he needs.   The daily discovery of indwelling corruption, inordinate affection—pride—self esteem—instability—love of
the world, and the innumerable other forms
which indwelling depravity assumes, endears to
him the fountain that cleanses from all sin—He
repairs afresh to it—washes again and again in
it, and these daily applications to the Atoning
blood makes sin increasingly sinful, and strength-
ens the panting of his soul for Divine conformity.

But, not so is it with the man who is a stranger to himself, while yet assenting with all the
vigour of a masculine intellect and an enlightened judgment to the truth of the doctrine of
Christ's atonement.  Reader, what is the atoning blood to you as far as its saving influence
extends, so long as you have never experienced
its power in your heart?  We charge you not
with an open hostility to this doctrine—we rank

you not among the number who profess no belief
whatever in its existence,—who deny it to be a
doctrine of revelation,—who refuse Divine honours to the person of the Redeemer, and trample
under foot His most precious Atoning blood—
we rank you not with this class of errorists.
You are in a sense, a *believer* in the Atonement
—you have always so believed in it—It has
always been an article of your orthodox creed.
You have never denied it—you have sat, and
still sit, beneath a ministry that holds it up to
view as the one hope of the sinner, the exclu-
sive ground of acceptance with GOD, and still
you are "dead in trespasses and in sins." What
an awful, and anomalous spectacle do you present! A *believer*, and yet an *unbeliever* in the
Atoning blood of Christ. *Receiving*, and yet *rejecting* it—*Consenting* to, and yet *denying* it—
*Vindicating* it and yet *turning your back* upon
it—your judgment *assenting* to it, your heart
*refusing* it!—What a spectacle do you present
to the whole intelligent universe—and to the
GOD of the universe! Bear with the writer while
he says it—he speaks with tenderness and affec-
*tion*—your intellectual reception of the doctrine

in question will avail you nothing while your
*heart* is yet a stranger to the experience of the
truth—Ah! you approve even of this—you assent
even to the justness of this remark. What is
your approval and your assent but, as the sign-
ing of your own death warrant?—See what an
alarming callousness a long life of impenitence,
and *Gospel preaching* has produced, that you
can cordially approve of the most solemn and
affecting statements—statements which bear
strongly upon your own condemnation, and yet
live on in a practical rejecting of Christ.

But, perhaps your reception of Christ in the
judgment—your long life of approval of His person and His work, have beguiled you into the
belief that you have really welcomed Him into
your heart—For this is not a mere hypothetical
case. There is such a thing as persuading
oneself into the belief that all is right, that the
heart is changed and heaven secured, from the
mere circumstance of the understanding being
enlightened. But let us examine for a moment
into this. You think you are converted, what
reason have you for thinking so? Upon what
grounds do you base this belief? Can you give

a reason with meekness and fear, of this supposed hope that is in you? Where is the evidence
of the mighty, spiritual, internal change? Has
that heart of yours ever been broken, softened,
humbled? Has it ever mourned over sin before
GOD? Have you ever sought and found a secret
place for repentance, confession and prayer?
Have your views of sin essentially altered? Do
you hate, abhor and loath it, and, is it the chief
cause of your daily sorrow? Are your views of
yourself materially changed? How does your
own righteousness appear to you? Are you
humble, meek, gentle? What is the precious
blood of the Saviour to you? Is it, with the
righteousness that justifies, all to your soul?
Are you living as a converted, regenerated man
—as a child of GOD—an heir of glory? Is your
life that of a cross bearing disciple of the Lord
Jesus—as one who is a stranger and a pilgrim
here—but, all whose hopes of honour and happiness are future and on high? But, is not your
history the very reverse of this? Be honest with
your soul and with GOD. Your decision now is
for the judgment and for eternity. Is not your
*whole life,* your daily walk—are not your pur-

suits and the governing principles of your conduct those of an individual yet unacquainted
with the experimental power of the truth? Is
there not a love of the world—a grasping for its
honours and its wealth, totally incompatible
with the humble, self-denying spirit of one professing to "love not the world nor the things of
the world," but, by the cross of Christ, to be
wholly crucified to it? These are solemn and
heart searching questions—And must, in a process of self examination, be frequently called up
in the court of conscience, and honestly and unequivocally answered by every true believer.
How much more anxiously ought he to weigh
these considerations and narrowly scrutinize
his heart, whose whole life to the present, has
been at variance with the first elements of the
Christian character.

We recur again to a former thought. To receive Christ, is not merely to cherish an inward
veneration, or to manifest an outward respect
for Him, His religion, His institutions or His
people. A man may talk well of Christ—think
highly of His disciples, His ministers, His laws,
and all the while live in a secret rebellion against

GOD, and a secret rejection of His Son.    "That
which is born of the flesh is flesh"—it is nothing but flesh—no elements of the spiritual nature are incorporated with it—it is flesh, all
flesh, and nothing but flesh; and yet, with this
fleshly nature, a man may speak well of Christ
—defend ably His cause, and outwardly profess
His name.

"The carnal mind is enmity against GOD."
It is nothing but enmity—no elements of love to
GOD are there—it is enmity, all enmity, and
nothing but enmity—neither, while it remains a
carnal mind, can it be otherwise.    And yet,
with this carnal mind a man may throw himself
in the very front ranks, and lead on the vanguard
of the host of GOD's elect.    O how solemn and
affecting is this thought.    May this train of remark have the tendency of driving the Christian
reader, not within himself in search of evidences,
proper as this, to a certain extent may be, but
to the feet of Jesus—to the cross of Christ—
there, viewing afresh His atoning blood, and all
sufficient righteousness, draw those evidences
from their proper and legitimate source—*the
finished work of Immanuel.*

The sin of rejecting the Saviour is, to the writer's mind, the sin of sins. The sin of thinking lightly of Christ, of turning the back upon GOD's unspeakable gift, of refusing to receive, love, and obey His only and well beloved Son is the sin which seems, like Aaron's rod, to swallow up every other. It is the master sin—the sin on which the great indictment will be made out against the ungodly world in the day when GOD shall make inquisition for blood. It is a sin too, shall we remind the impenitent reader, of which the devils have never been guilty! To them the Saviour has never been sent. Before their eyes the cross has never been lifted. Along their gloomy coasts no tidings of redeeming mercy have ever echoed. To reject the Saviour then —to turn your back upon the cross,—to heed not the glad tidings of redemption, and to *die* in that state, is to pass to the judgment guilty of a sin, from the charge of which even Satan himself will be acquitted! "This is the condemnation that light is come into the world, and men love darkness rather than light, because their deeds are evil."

The reason of this will be obvious to a thought-

·ful mind. No where has GOD made such a full
and glorious revelation of Himself, as He has
done in sending His only begotten and well beloved Son into the world. All the glory of all
creation—worlds on worlds and suns on suns—
and all the glory of providence collected as into
one focus, would possess no glory by reason of
the glory that excels in the incarnation, obedience and death of the Lord Jesus Christ. Here
JEHOVAH, as it were, comes forth from the pa-
vilion of His greatness, and unveiling His glories, shews Himself to man. Here, all the perfections and attributes of the Divine character
are revealed. And here too, *love*, the crowning
attribute of all, shines with surpassing lustre.
May it not be lawful to ask—without limiting
the power of Omnipotence—whether it were
possible for JEHOVAH to have devised a method
better fitted to make Himself known to His
creatures than the mission of His Son into our
world? The incarnation of Deity is an amazing
theme. The thought of this could have originated but with Deity Himself. The united
strength of all created intellect would never have
*devised* this plan of revealing the Divine glo-

ries, and making known the divine mind. It
was meet that it should originate with GOD and
Him only. What angel in heaven, even had
the idea been conceived in his mind, would have
breathed the proposal that GOD should become
incarnate and so die for man? O no, it was too
grand a thought for created mind.

Now, let the impenitent reader consider solemnly the fearful sin, and weigh well the appalling consequences, of rejecting the Lord Jesus
Christ. In rejecting Christ, you turn your back
upon GOD Himself. Has He not declared it?
How then are we to interpret these solemn
words? "He that hateth me hateth my Father
also." John, xv. 23. "For the Father judgeth
no man, but hath committed all judgment unto
the Son. That all men should honour the Son,
even as they honour the Father. He that honoureth not the Son honoureth not the Father which
hath sent Him." John, v. 22, 23. Behold in what
light the word of truth places the sin of hating, honouring not, and rejecting the Lord Jesus, the
Son of GOD, and the Redeemer of men. We
beseech you, ponder well the sin of turning your
back upon GOD's "unspeakable gift."

Permit us for a moment to glance at the *pre-sent* consequences—consequences felt in this life—of rejecting Christ. A stranger experimentally to the atoning blood, your heart must necessarily be a stranger to true *happiness.* Knowing nothing of a state of reconciliation, your mind can know nothing of the *peace* of GOD. You may repair to the ball room and frequent the theatre ;—You may visit the scenes of fashionable gaiety, or you may descend to the regions of guilty pleasure, and there, excitement may flutter your heart and flush your cheek, and impart a moment's radiance to your eye, and yet, the truth of GOD's word is verified in your experience—"THERE IS NO PEACE SAITH MY GOD TO THE WICKED." Isa. lviii.21. Talk of happiness to the culprit within the grasp of the law—speak of peace to the man under the condemnation of death, and as soon might you expect a response from his heart, as from his, who is living a rebel against GOD, and a stranger to the atoning and peace speaking blood of Christ. O no, reader—you will ever be a stranger to true peace, you will know nothing of true happiness *until you* find it at the foot of the cross—in a sense of pardon—reconciliation and acceptance with God. The world will deceive you—and sin will deceive you—and Satan will deceive you, and your own heart will deceive you, and even friends may deceive you,—all speaking "peace, peace" when there is no peace—but heed them not. Go you as a sinner lost, a sinner undone, a sinner without ought but your vileness to commend you, and wash in the fountain open for all sin—and thus repenting, and believing in Jesus, your "peace shall be as a river and your righteousness as the waves of the sea."

The *remoter* consequences of rejecting the Atonement of Christ are almost of too fearful a character to trace out. And yet the word of God is our guide in this, as on all other matters, connected with the welfare, present and eternal, of the undying soul. We open it, and we read of "everlasting punishment"—"the worm that never dies and the fire that is never quenched," of "everlasting torments," of "everlasting destruction from the presence of the Lord and from the glory of his power," of "everlasting fire prepared for the devil and his angels," of "outer darkness where there is weeping and wailing

21*

and gnashing of teeth." All this, and more,
we read in connexion with the final state
of the impenitent and unbelieving, the rejector
of the Atonement of the Son of God. And is it
surprizing that this should be thy doom sinner?
Not, if it be remembered that, a rejection of
Christ's Atonement involves a rejection of the
*only* way of salvation. "Other foundation can
no man lay than that is laid which is Jesus
Christ." 1 Cor. iii. 11. "Neither is there salvation in any other: for there is none other
name under heaven given among men, whereby
we must be saved." Acts, iv. 12. "There remaineth no more sacrifice for sin, but a fearful
looking for of judgment and fiery indignation
which shall devour the adversaries." If this
be true—and most true it is—to what an alarming state, is the sinner reduced! He must receive Christ or be eternally banished from heaven. This is the only plank, reject this, and
your soul must sink beneath the dark billows of
Jehovah's wrath. Then, what ought to be your
present course? Immediate repentance and humiliation before God—This must be your first
*step*—Throw down the weapons of your long

rebellion—ground your arms before the cross—
and come in the posture and with the confession,
of a law condemned and self condemned soul.
Think not of a *future* repentance—dream not of
a death bed conversion—it is a work too great
and important to leave until then—It must be
done *now*—the *present* is yours only—*Tomorrow*
you may be in eternity. Many have been the
sermons you have heard—solemn have been the
warnings you have received—affecting have
been the entreaties and motives with which the
faithful minister, and the beseeching parent, and
the anxious friend have plied you,—and yet you
remain impenitent and unbelieving. Repent then,
this moment repent—"GOD commands" you to
repent ; death, judgment, eternity all urge you to
repent *now*—Think not that you have ought of
goodness to commend you to GOD. On His
mercy you have no possible *claim*. You richly
*deserve* to die. And it is a wonder of wonders
that you are at this moment out of hell. O, trifle
not with the long suffering patience of GOD. It
may weary soon, and then He will swear that
you, who have broken His law—slighted His
grace—and rejected His Son shall never enter

into His rest. But, if you are resolved to perish in your impenitence and unbelief—If you
are resolved to die rejecting Christ and His
great salvation—If you have made a covenant
with death, and with hell are at an agreement,
then, there remaineth no more sacrifice for sin,
but one tremendous, appalling alternative.—O it
is a fearful one, pause ere you choose it—the
alternative of being eternally damned!

THE END.

Printed in the USA
CPSIA information can be obtained
at www.ICGtesting.com
LVHW041235010624
781915LV00001B/44